Teaching Word Recognition

WHAT WORKS FOR SPECIAL-NEEDS LEARNERS
Karen R. Harris and Steve Graham
Editors

Strategy Instruction for Students with Learning Disabilities
Robert Reid and Torri Ortiz Lienemann

Teaching Mathematics to Middle School Students
with Learning Difficulties
Marjorie Montague and Asha K. Jitendra, Editors

Teaching Word Recognition: Effective Strategies for Students
with Learning Difficulties
Rollanda E. O'Connor

Teaching Reading Comprehension to Students with Learning Difficulties
Janette K. Klingner, Sharon Vaughn, and Alison Boardman

Teaching Word Recognition

Effective Strategies for Students with Learning Difficulties

Rollanda E. O'Connor

Series Editors' Note by Karen R. Harris and Steve Graham

THE GUILFORD PRESS
New York   London

©2007 The Guilford Press
A Division of Guilford Publications, Inc.
72 Spring Street, New York, NY 10012
www.guilford.com

Printed in the United States of America

This book is printed on acid-free paper.

Last digit is print number: 9 8 7 6 5 4 3 2 1

Library of Congress Cataloging-in-Publication Data

O'Connor, Rollanda E.
    Teaching word recognition : effective strategies for students with
learning difficulties / by Rollanda E. O'Connor.
        p. cm. — (What works for special-needs learners)
    Includes bibliographical references and index.
    ISBN-13: 978-1-59385-364-8 ISBN-10: 1-59385-364-5 (pbk.: alk. paper)
    ISBN-13: 978-1-59385-365-5 ISBN-10: 1-59385-365-3 (cloth: alk. paper)
    1. Reading comprehension.   2. Learning disabled children—Education.
3. Language arts (Elementary)   I. Title.
LB1050.45.O26 2006
372.46′2—dc22
                                                                            2006027887

To Daniel Edward O'Connor, with gratitude and love

About the Author

Rollanda E. O'Connor, PhD, is a reading specialist and Professor in the Graduate School of Education at the University of California, Riverside. Before joining the university, she taught reading in special and general education classrooms for many years. Since then, Dr. O'Connor's research has centered on issues of reading acquisition and reading improvement. She has conducted numerous reading intervention studies in general and special education settings, examined procedures to predict the students most likely to develop reading disabilities, and followed the reading progress of students who have received early intervention. Her longitudinal studies of intervention and assessment led to the development of *Ladders to Literacy* (1998/2005), a collection of phonological and print awareness activities and scaffolding suggestions for children at risk for reading problems. Dr. O'Connor's current research includes exploring the effects of early, continuous intervention across the first 4 years of reading development and developing research-based interventions for students with reading difficulties in the intermediate grades.

Series Editors' Note

After eating at a fabulous Chinese restaurant, a young lady of Chinese descent told her mother she should try it. When her mother asked for the name of the restaurant, the young woman said she thought it was printed on the front door. She wrote the Chinese character down and asked, "Mom, can you tell me the restaurant's name?" Her mother laughed and then replied, "Pull."

This story illustrates a simple but powerful fact: If you cannot read words, you cannot access the meaning of written text. Unfortunately, too many children experience difficulty mastering this fundamental skill. *Teaching Word Recognition: Effective Strategies for Students with Learning Difficulties* by Rollanda E. O'Connor provides an antidote to this problem by giving teachers and other practitioners validated instructional techniques for teaching the skills involved in reading words to students with learning difficulties.

This book is part of the series What Works for Special-Needs Learners. This series addresses a significant need in the education of learners with special needs—students who are at risk, those with disabilities, and all children and adolescents who struggle with learning or behavior. Researchers in special education, educational psychology, curriculum and instruction, and other fields have made great progress in understanding what works for struggling learners, yet the practical application of this research base remains quite limited. This is due in part to the lack of appropriate materials for teachers, teacher educators, and inservice teacher development programs. Books in this series present assessment, instructional, and classroom management methods with a strong research base and provide specific "how-to" instructions and examples of the use of proven procedures in schools.

Teaching Word Recognition presents instructional techniques and activities that are scientifically validated, moving from the beginning stages through skilled word reading. These evidence-based practices provide teachers with the tools they need to make sure all of their students master the process of reading words. An invaluable resource for practitioners, this book is also suitable for use in reading methods courses and coursework in the area of learning disabilities and reading disabilities.

Future books in the series will cover such issues as reading comprehension, vocabulary instruction, self-determination, social skills instruction, writing, and working with families. All volumes will be as thorough and detailed as the present one and will facilitate implementation of evidence-based practices in classrooms and schools.

KAREN R. HARRIS
STEVE GRAHAM

Contents

Introduction

Learning to read is the single most important academic task of the elementary school years; however, many of our school children fail in this task. This is a book about reading words. It may seem strange to focus a book on reading individual words when the intent behind learning to read is to comprehend sentences, paragraphs, and pages of connected words. Nevertheless, the recognition of printed words is the largest barrier in the reading process for children with reading disabilities as well as other children who struggle to keep up with their peers in the acquisition of this critical academic skill.

One might think that teaching students to read words would be much easier than teaching students the meanings of the words or ways to comprehend what they read, but teachers report that their lack of knowledge in teaching word identification is a major instructional stumbling block as they plan their reading lessons (Bos, Mather, Silver-Pacuilla, & Narr, 2000; McCutchen & Berninger, 1999). Observations of reading instruction in classrooms substantiate this confusion over just how to go about teaching children to get those words off the page. Researchers who watch teachers teach reading find few instances of instruction that demonstrates how to analyze words, how to break words into manageable parts, and how to put the parts together to produce a word (Juel & Minden-Cupp, 2000; Vaughn, Moody, & Schumm, 1998).

This book is designed to address this state of affairs by synthesizing the research on reading words from the very beginning stages through skilled word reading. Along with the research, the teaching techniques and activities that have been most effective are described, so that teachers can implement these best practices in their daily instruction. The good news is that studies have shown consistently that teachers can improve students' academic outcomes by improving their own instructional practices (Darling-Hammond, 2000). Of course, skilled reading is the result of multiple factors, which include features of the home environment, parenting, and genetics, but the strongest influence on how well students read is the instruction they receive after they enter school. When students learn new skills and strategies for reading that build upon others they have learned, they can make rapid gains in reading whether they learn the new skills through early intervention or after a diagnosis of reading disability has been made (Ehri & McCormick, 1998). Because instruction is central to the reading development of most students, this book is focused on the kinds of instruction that improve students' ability to read words and to become competent readers.

The purpose of this book is to help students with learning disabilities and other struggling readers to attain a level of word recognition that makes reading (1) functional for gaining information, (2) enjoyable, so that students choose to read for pleasure, and (3) efficient when reading silently or to others. Chapter by chapter, the skills addressed in this book will lead teachers through the kinds of activities that enable students to build an intricate and flexible framework for reading all kinds of words.

Each strategy introduced here has been tested in scientific studies and will help teachers plan and teach a coordinated series of lessons that can bring about rapid improvements in students' reading. Teachers should note that the methods, strategies, and overall approaches in each chapter have been researched and validated in experimental studies that included students who were very hard to teach. Table I.1 shows the progression of skills that contribute to reading words, along with the place in this book where the skill and instructional strategies to teach it are described. Below, the overall framework for the information in each chapter is summarized.

THE PROGRESSION FROM ORAL LANGUAGE TO READING COMPREHENSION

Before leading students down the road toward skilled reading of words, it may be useful to consider how reading develops. The purpose of learning to read and write is to enable communication from a distance, but the language that facilitates reading begins as face-to-face communication.

Oral Language

Communication begins as children recognize and understand the meanings of nonverbal cues, such as facial expressions and gestures, and grows as children understand the words used by their parents and caregivers. Children gradually develop their ability to use words to express their desires and to comment on the world

TABLE I.1. Scientifically Validated Reading Strategies and Where to Find Them

Strategy	Description	It helps the reader:	Location
Expanding the child's words	The adult follows the child's interests and engages in conversations centered on current objects and events.	Use descriptive language and learn new words.	Chapter 1
Text Talk	The adult invites conversation from the child as they read a book together.	Learn grammatical phrasing and the meanings of words.	Chapter 1
Dialogic reading	The adult asks questions about the pictures and text as the child listens and comments.	Anticipate story structure and events and mimic the author's phrasing.	Chapter 1
Stretched segmenting	Children learn to say one-syllable words slowly.	Hear each speech sound in the word.	Chapter 2
Stretched blending	The teacher shows children four pictures or objects, and says a word slowly. Children blend the speech sounds together to say the word fast.	Synthesize speech sounds into recognizable words.	Chapter 2
Isolating the first sound	The teacher demonstrates how to listen for the first sound in words.	Hear single phonemes that begin words and begin to use inventive spelling.	Chapter 2
Isolating the last sound	The teacher demonstrates how to listen for the last sound in words.	Hear single phonemes that end words and begin to use inventive spelling.	Chapter 2
Isolating the middle sound	The teacher demonstrates how to listen for the medial sound in words.	Hear single phonemes in the middle of words and begin to use correct spelling.	Chapter 2
Segmenting words into all of their phonemes	The teacher uses visual guidance to help students break one-syllable words into each phoneme in sequence.	Link written and spoken forms of words and spell.	Chapter 2
Integrating phonemic awareness with letters	The teacher demonstrates how learned letter sounds can be matched to the first sound that children hear in words.	Understand and use the alphabetic principle.	Chapter 3
Phoneme identity	The teacher demonstrates how learned letter sounds can be matched to the sounds in various positions in words.	Understand that sounds can occur in many positions in words.	Chapter 3
Inventive spelling	The teacher encourages children to attempt spellings of words they have not learned to spell.	Apprehend the process of spelling words.	Chapter 3

(continued)

TABLE I.1. *(continued)*

Strategy	Description	It helps the reader:	Location
Segment-to-spell	The teacher demonstrates how to capture a complete spelling by matching known letter sounds to phonemes in words.	Link knowledge of segmenting and blending to reading.	Chapter 3
Filling in the blanks	The teacher encourages children to write messages in which only one or two words are written by the children.	Integrate reading and writing as reciprocal processes.	Chapter 3
Cumulative introduction of letters and sounds	The teacher introduces only one new letter in an instructional session and continues to review all known letters each day.	Learn the new letter–sound pair while retaining previously learned letters and sounds.	Chapter 4
Blending letter sounds in words	The teacher demonstrates how to stretch each letter sound until the entire word has been decoded.	Rely on the sounds in words to generate a pronunciation.	Chapter 4
Blending the consonant with the vowel	Children say the vowel sound first, combine it with the initial consonant, and then blend the two phonemes with the ending sounds.	Avoid adding a schwa sound with the initial consonant.	Chapter 4
Examining minimal pairs	Children change one letter at a time in a string of words to change one word into another word.	Notice the difference in word identity caused by changing a single letter.	Chapter 4
Teaching letter patterns	Teachers use cumulative introduction to teach the most common and consistent letter patterns in words.	Use two- and three-letter patterns to decode unknown words.	Chapter 5
The silent-*e* rule	Teachers demonstrate how the final *e* functions in words.	Learn when to use short or long vowel sounds to read words.	Chapter 5
Constant time delay	Teachers create a set of five new words and provide modeled practice trials in which they read the word and have students wait 3 seconds before reading it.	Recognize words that occur frequently quickly.	Chapter 6
Spelling words aloud	Teachers direct students to spell a word aloud as the students examine the word.	Notice all of the letters in a word in sequence.	Chapter 6

(continued)

TABLE I.1. *(continued)*

Strategy	Description	It helps the reader:	Location
Sets of words with unusual spellings	Teachers cluster high-frequency words that share a spelling pattern, such as *could*, *would*, and *should*, and point out the memorable similarity.	Recognize unusual spelling patterns quickly.	Chapter 6
Word walls and word banks	Teachers display learned words by organizing them in alphabetical lists on the classroom wall or in a word card box.	Practice words that were learned previously.	Chapter 6
Practicing games for sight words	Teachers use sets of learned words in small group games such as Concentration, Bingo, or Beat the Clock.	Retain words that were learned previously.	Chapter 6
Cover and connect	Teachers demonstrate how to cover a word ending to read a base word and how to reconnect the ending to the base word.	Break apart and reassemble words with two syllables.	Chapter 7
Recognizing affixes in words	Teachers teach students to identify and read the most common prefixes and suffixes that occur in words.	Read and understand the meanings of multisyllable words.	Chapter 7
Using vowels to break words into syllables	Teachers demonstrate the rule that each syllable has at least one vowel.	Predict the number of syllables a word will have.	Chapter 7
Dividing words between consonants	Teachers direct students to underline the vowels in two-syllable words as above, then show how to try pronunciations by dividing syllables between consonants.	Predict number of syllables and identify likely dividing points between them.	Chapter 7
Identifying syllable types	Teachers provide a week or more of practice on identifying each of the syllable types in English.	Pronounce the vowels correctly in long words.	Chapter 7
BEST a multisyllable word	Teachers rehearse the acronym (B = Break the word apart, E = Examine the parts, S = Say each part, T = Try the whole thing) and show students how to apply it to long words.	Decode words with several syllables.	Chapter 7

(continued)

TABLE I.1. (continued)

Strategy	Description	It helps the reader:	Location
Generating word webs	Teachers lead students naming multiple forms of words by brainstorming affixes.	Quickly locate where affixes have been added to base words.	Chapter 7
Dropping the silent *e*	Teachers lead students to practice the rule for dropping the silent *e* when they are adding a suffix that begins with a vowel.	Recognize when *e*'s have been dropped in words, which helps to generate a correct pronunciation for a vowel.	Chapter 7
Doubling a consonant	Teachers show students how to identify the conditions in which final consonants must be doubled, as in *stopped* or *preferred*.	Pronounce vowels correctly in long words and spell words with endings correctly.	Chapter 7
Changing -*y* to -*i*	Teachers lead students to practice the rule in which we change the *y* to *i* if words end in a consonant +*y*.	Identify base words where *y*'s have been changed.	Chapter 7
Rereading	Teachers listen to and time students' oral reading of a passage several times until students increase their reading rate by 25% or more.	Read faster with fewer errors and more appropriate phrasing.	Chapter 8
Partner reading (Classwide Peer Tutoring and PALS)	Teachers pair students in the class to read aloud to each other for 10–20 minutes several times a week.	Read faster with fewer errors and more appropriate phrasing.	Chapter 8

around them. Most children enter school with more than 2,000 words in their speaking vocabularies, and their rate of learning new words increases over the first few years of school. Nevertheless, for oral language to contribute to reading and writing during kindergarten and first grade, we need to ask children (or teach them how, if they cannot already do so) to backtrack in their development and to think of words not only as meaningful referents to their worlds and thoughts, but as collections of sounds—much as they did as infants trying to capture speech sounds in the words they heard.

Phonemic Awareness

Why would we ask children to revert to this focus on sounds within words? Because reading and writing depend on children understanding that words are sequential collections of speech sounds (National Reading Panel, 2000). Each speech sound (e.g., the sounds made by the letters *f*, *i*, and *sh* in *fish*) is called a phoneme. Phonemic awareness is the ability to hear and manipulate the speech sounds in words, as when children generate a rhyme with another word or pick out the first or last sound in a spoken word. When children attempt to read a word that they do not immediately know how to pronounce, they generate a sound (a phoneme) for each letter that they see and blend those phonemes together. The flip side of phonemic blending is phonemic segmentation, which is the basis for spelling. Children attempt to spell a word by identifying all of the sounds (phonemes) they hear and then by trying to match each sound to an alphabet letter. Blending and segmenting are the core skills of phonemic awareness and are discussed and demonstrated in Chapter 2.

The Alphabetic Principle

Hearing the speech sounds in words (phonemic awareness) provides a good start toward reading, but unless children also know many of the letters of the alphabet and the sounds they tend to make in the spellings of words, they will make poor progress in learning to read. The phonemes of our speech are represented by letters or collections of letters in our alphabet. By understanding the link between speech sounds in spoken words and alphabet letters and letter combinations in written words, children learn to read and spell. The alphabetic principle is the focus of Chapter 3.

Decoding Words

One of the major tasks of the reading teacher in kindergarten and first grade is to ensure that children learn all of the common letter sounds and letter combinations and how to blend these sounds together when they see printed words. The blending of letter sounds to generate pronunciations of written words is called decoding. Teachers are sometimes troubled by the laborious transformation of letters to sounds by beginning readers. Nevertheless, this letter–sound-by-letter–sound decoding provides children with the tool to read a word that they have never encountered in print before. Teaching children to decode words is the focus of Chapters 4 and 5.

Words with Irregular Spellings and Multiple Syllables

By the time children decode a word several times, they begin to recognize it faster, without needing to decode consciously, although they still attend to each letter in the word. If the letters are so important, how can children read words where letters make unusual sounds, such as in *laugh* or *yacht*? Some of these words are learned through memorization without analysis, especially when they occur very frequently in sentences and stories (words such as *one* and *two*, for example). For words that occur less frequently, children use clues in the spellings and sentence context to match a probable pronunciation of a printed word to a word in their speaking and listening vocabulary. Long words present particular problems for children because the decoding rules that worked for reading short words often do not work with multisyllabic words. For long words, children need to learn common affixes, such as *pre-*, *un-*, *-able*, and *-ion*. Moreover, they need to learn more flexible strategies for trying out alternative pronunciations. A richer store of words in children's oral language provides children with more possibilities. Teaching children to read irregularly spelled and long words is the focus of Chapters 6 and 7.

Reading Fluency

This book is all about reading words, but children need to read them effortlessly as well as accurately so that the sentences and paragraphs on the page come to life. For many children, building a comfortable rate of reading provides additional challenges. Although for many years rate of reading was believed to be relatively unimportant, we now realize the strong relationship between reading rate and reading comprehension, and so this challenge must be faced and overcome for children to achieve reading's ultimate aim of communicating the thoughts of the writer. Methods that have been empirically validated for improving reading fluency are introduced in Chapter 8.

Older Students with Reading Difficulties

Most of the chapters of this book will be useful for teachers in the early grades who are responsible for building a strong foundation of reading skills in the children they teach. Unfortunately, not all children learn to read well in the primary grades. Moreover, the popular press suggests that if children do not learn to read well by third grade, it may be too late to teach them to read at all. Fortunately, a growing body of research with older students suggests just the opposite. Many of the same techniques we recommend for teaching beginning readers can be used effectively with students in fourth grade and beyond and with similar results. The research support and the methods for improving older students' ability to read words are presented in Chapter 9.

USING THIS BOOK

The book is arranged in the order in which the reading skills most related to word recognition unfold for typical readers. The first three chapters provide a framework that is useful for children with and without disabilities in general or special education kindergarten and first-grade classrooms. The research and strategies in Chapters 2 and 3 are also useful in remedial contexts for students who are far behind grade-level expectations for reading progress. Resources for teaching older students, along with other materials described throughout this book, are located in Appendix A.

Teachers will want to assess older students to determine which components of reading have been learned already and a good starting point for teaching students to identify printed words. Checklists for informal assessment of skills can be found in Appendix B. Although this book is about reading words, there is much more to reading well than reading words. Teachers should integrate the instructional strategies in this book with instruction that develops students' vocabulary, reading comprehension, spelling, and writing to develop the kind of literacy that can support students' lifelong learning opportunities.

CHAPTER 1

In the Beginning

Oral Language and Learning to Read Words

Learning to read is a developmental process that draws upon all that children have learned about language. It is obvious that reading comprehension relies on understanding speech, which relies on understanding the meanings of words (vocabulary) and acceptable sentence forms (syntax), and that comprehension of language begins to emerge in the first few years of life. More recently, we have begun to understand how oral language also contributes to children's ability to read words as well as to comprehend them.

As children learn to read, they concentrate laboriously on deciphering the words that form the text of sentences. Teachers assume that when text is simple children can use their oral-language abilities to work out the meaning of those sentences. That is not an improper assumption because, even in adults, listening comprehension accounts for most of the variation in reading comprehension (Palmer, MacLeod, Hunt, & Davidson, 1985). Because oral language, reading words, and reading comprehension are intimately intertwined, I begin this book with a discussion of how language contributes to reading development and how reading development contributes to the increasingly complex forms of children's oral language. The chapter ends with research-based recommendations for how teachers can improve the oral-language abilities of their students.

Oral language has its origins in mimicry and play. Children babble within a few months of life, and their babbling soon approximates the speech sounds of the languages they hear. The infant tries "ba-ba-ba," and the parent eagerly mimics back "ba-ba" to reinforce the baby's attempt at communication and to shape the syllables toward the real word, *bottle.* The more the adults and children who surround the infant imitate and engage the infant in these early attempts to communicate, the earlier the child is likely to use discernible words. As young children learn to understand and say approximate pronunciations of words, they begin to name objects in the world around them. From objects, children link names to actions and desires, and the charming babble of the infant becomes communication. Between 2 and 4 years of age, most children show dramatic growth in language, particularly in understanding the meanings of words, their interrelationships, and grammatical forms (Scarborough, 2001).

Language experts estimate that, on average, children acquire roughly 2,500 words on their own as speaking vocabulary prior to entering kindergarten (Owens, 1999), which is a very good thing because most children in kindergarten love to communicate. In the sections that follow, I lay out the ways in which speaking and listening contribute to reading development.

THE CONTRIBUTION OF ORAL LANGUAGE TO READING AND COMPREHENDING WORDS

The transition from speaking and listening to reading and writing is not a smooth one for many children. Although a well-developed vocabulary can make that transition easier, many children also have difficulty learning the production and meanings of words. To understand how difficult acquiring language can be, Catts and Kamhi (1999) define five parameters of language that work both independently and collaboratively as children learn the meanings of words. These parameters include phonology (speech sounds of language), semantics (meanings of words and phrases), morphology (meaningful parts of words and word tenses), syntax (rules for combining and ordering words in phrases), and pragmatics (appropriate use of language in context). The first three (phonology, semantics, and morphology) combine to enable development of listening and speaking vocabulary, but they also contribute independently to children's ability to read individual words. All five of these language features contribute to children's ability to understand sentences, whether the sentence is heard or read.

If children understand what they hear and can translate printed words into speech, then they can use their listening comprehension to enable reading comprehension. For good readers in fourth grade and beyond, levels of reading comprehension and listening comprehension are roughly equivalent, and each kind of comprehension facilitates the other (Nippold, 1998). Much of this comprehension is based on understanding the meanings of words and phrases, and children's level of vocabulary knowledge is a good predictor of their reading comprehension (Hargrave & Senechal, 2000; Snow, Tabors, & Dickinson, 2001). Because of the robustness of this relationship, Gough and his colleagues (Gough & Tunmer, 1986; Hoover & Gough, 1990) have proposed the "simple view of reading," in which reading consists of two components: reading words and listening comprehension (of words, phrases, and sentences). In this view, children's oral language, combined with their ability to read words, generates the basis for reading comprehension.

In addition to facilitating comprehension, some aspects of oral language also contribute directly to reading words. Children with larger speaking vocabularies in preschool may have an easier time with phoneme awareness and the alphabetic principle because they can draw on more words to explore the similarities among the sounds they hear in spoken words and the letters that form the words (Metsala & Walley, 1998). More recently, researchers have also suggested that children with larger vocabularies find it easier to read words that have unusual spellings (Ehri, 2005). For example, to read a word like *bread*, children may sound out /br/-/ee/-/d/ (decoding a word), decide that *breed* does not make sense in the sentence (oral-language comprehension), and replace *breed* with a word they know that does make sense (i.e., *bread*) and also shares some of the word's print characteristics such as the *br* at the beginning and the *d* at the end. Without a mental store of words to match the printed and spoken word against, children will have difficulty reading words with unusual spellings.

Oral language influences reading ability in different ways at different stages of reading development and may play a greater role as comprehension assumes a greater share of the reading process (Carver, 2003). As mentioned earlier, young children with larger speaking and listening vocabularies find it easier to acquire awareness of the speech sounds in words, and this phoneme awareness directly influences acquisition of word decoding ability, which in turn increases access to print (Perfetti, 2003). During the primary grades, children who read develop more knowledge of the world alongside larger, more connected vocabularies, both of which improve reading comprehension (Stanovich, 2000). The empirical support for the link between vocabulary and reading comprehension has been well established (McKeown, Beck, Omanson, & Pople, 1985). In fact, reading comprehension depends on high-quality understanding of the meanings of words as well as the ability to read them (Perfetti & Hart, 2002).

Although children can learn to read words in kindergarten and first grade even with impoverished speaking vocabularies (O'Connor, Notari-Syverson, & Vadasy, 1996, 1998), understanding print requires extensive experience with oral language. Evidence suggests that size of vocabulary in preschool influences reading development by enabling children to consider the meanings of word parts (Metsala & Walley, 1998). For example, if a child knows the meanings of *ball* and *basket*, then *basketball* is learned as an independent word and also as a meaningful combination of its two smaller parts.

Decoding, however, relies less on understanding spoken words and more on the instruction that children receive in phoneme blending and segmenting, in the sounds of alphabet letters, and in how to combine that knowledge into a process for translating printed words into spoken words. This distinction is important because reading words and acquiring word meanings (vocabulary) appear to be complementary activities that work in a reciprocal fashion. Teaching students to read words can assist in the development of oral language and vocabulary, as well as the other way around (Connor, Morrison, & Katch, 2004). When children are able to release words from printed text, reading becomes easier, they read more, and reading more exposes them to more new words, new phrasing, decontextualized language, figures of speech, and syntax outside the range of their everyday speaking and listening vocabularies (Swanborn & de Glopper, 1999). So, a large vocabulary helps children to read words, and reading more words helps to build vocabulary, which in turns makes reading words easier, and so forth.

STORYBOOKS AND ORAL LANGUAGE

Given the relationship between oral language and comprehending written words, it only makes sense to do all we can as teachers and parents to help children begin their schooling with a strong speaking and listening vocabulary. Unfortunately, not all children have equal opportunity to learn the meanings and usages of words. Home environment contributes to opportunity to learn (Payne, Whitehurst, & Angell, 1994) and differences between the vocabulary size of children from high- and low-income households have been documented in many studies (National Research Council, 2002). On average, children who are raised in higher-income households own more books and have more opportunity for prolonged conversation with adults that includes a rich store of unfamiliar words (Snow, Tabors, Nicholson, & Kurland, 1995). The vocabularies of children are strongly related to those of their parents (Hart & Risley, 1995). Nevertheless, access to books and conversation need not be limited by the socioeconomic level of a family, and even small improvements in home literacy environment can have especially strong effects for children who are raised in low-income households (Dearing, McCartney, & Taylor, 2001).

One of the best-documented methods for improving the vocabularies of children prior to school entry is through interactive storybook reading between children and their caregivers. Two theories on how reading with children improves oral language have been supported through research. In one theory, the child's vocabulary improves as a result of the conversations between the child and the caregiver who reads the story (Weizman & Snow, 2001). These conversations are developed through dialogic storybook reading (Whitehurst et al., 1988), in which the caregiver encourages the child to use the language possibilities of storybooks by following his or her interests. Children point out features of illustrations and ask the reader questions about them, which may or may not be part of the central story of the text. Children label these features and attach descriptive words to them. The book serves as a stimulus for conversation outside the immediate context, introducing words that are less familiar, and children have opportunities to incorporate these words into book-centered conversations.

When books are read repeatedly, these descriptions can be revisited and elaborated. The child becomes familiar with the story's vocabulary and begins to anticipate the storyline. Bus and colleagues (Bus, Belsky, van IJzendoorn, & Crnik, 1997; Bus, van IJzendoorn, & Pellegrini, 1995) suggest that the story that is told interactively between the child and the reader may vary considerably from the printed story, depending on the child's interests and the reader's responsiveness to those interests. Pursuing the child's interests provides a motivational dimension to the conversation that can make new vocabulary more memorable to the child.

In an alternative but complementary theory, van Kleek (2004) suggests that sharing books provides the kind of invariant routine that many young children need in order to acquire language outside of day-to-day interactions. When storybooks are read over and over, caregivers offer children the experience of using language that is at a higher or more formal level than speech, either in repeating responses of particular characters, in role plays, or in storytelling, in which children use the pictures of the book as clues to deliver a pretend reading that is quite close to the author's rendering of the story. Teachers note that following several readings of a story, children who cannot yet read independently often take the book into a corner of the room and "read" it to themselves and their peers, adopting the book's language as their own (Adger, Hoyle, & Dickinson, 2004).

Children develop language through repeated routines. For children with developmental delays, routines help them acquire language and use it more intelligibly (van Kleek, 2004). One advantage of rereading books to children is that the routine is more stable than the time of day or the event of sitting with an adult with a book as the source of attention. The book is the same each time it is read, and through this repetitive sameness children not only learn language, but also conventions about book handling, including the concept of the printed word and its invariance over time. An example of how adults can use storybooks to stimulate children's oral-language development is shown below.

Storybook Reading (*The Teddy Bears' Picnic* by Kennedy & Theobalds) with Preschool and Kindergarten Children

PARENT OR TEACHER	CHILD
If you go down to the woods today you're sure of a big surprise. Yes, that sign points the way to the woods. If you go down to the woods today you'd better go in disguise. Uh-oh (*points to the boy with the large hat over his face*), he's all wrapped up so you can't recognize him.	(*Points to the sign.*) The woods!
	Just-guys.
Yes, he's wearing a disguise. When he wears clothes that make it hard to know who he is, he's in disguise. (*Says each syllable distinctly.*)	Disguise. He has a big hat. That's disguise.

It's almost Halloween, and you'll wear a disguise.	No, I'll wear a costume for Halloween.
A costume is like a disguise. When you wear your costume, nobody will know who *you* are. The costume will disguise you. Yes, you'll be disguised as Superman.	I'll wear a disguise. I'll be Superman.
(*Turns page.*) Look at all those bears!	
(*They sing together.*) For every bear that ever there was	(*They sing together.*) For every bear that ever there was
Will gather there for certain because	Will gather there for certain because
Today's the day the teddy bears have their picnic.	Today's the day the teddy bears have their picnic.
(*Turns page.*) Ev'ry teddy bear who's been good is sure of a treat today.	I can count the bears: 1–2–3–4–5–6–7–8 . . .
That's a lot of bears! That's an enormous number of bears.	Enormous number. Lots of bears, huh.
(*Turns page.*) There's lots of marvelous things to eat.	
(*Points at picture.*) Look at all that yummy food. This will be a marvelous picnic.	(*Points to the cake, the pie, the cookies.*) That's marvelous and that's marvelous and that's marvelous . . .

Regardless of which theory is more useful for explaining how language develops from storybook reading, it is clear that vocabulary improves as a result of the experience. For typically developing 2-year-olds, about 5% of their daily speech is acquired through storybook reading with older siblings and adults (Wells, 1985).

The language development that occurs through children's interactions with parents is clearly important, but teachers also have an impact on children's language development. Huttenlocher, Vasileva, Cymerman, and Levine (2002) assessed the unique effects of home and school environments on language and found that preschool teachers can positively influence language growth in addition to improvements attributed to the child's home environment. This impact was especially strong for the children most in need of improvement, a finding echoed in kindergarten classrooms (Dickinson, 2001; O'Connor et al., 1996; Payne et al., 1994). The importance of fostering early language development is evident in longitudinal studies in which receptive language in kindergarten strongly predicted seventh-grade reading comprehension (Dickinson & Tabors, 2001).

Although poorly developed oral vocabulary has been considered a serious impediment to learning to read, recent studies have provided good news for teachers, in that children who begin school with poorly developed vocabulary can make large vocabulary gains in kindergarten when instruction includes interactive book reading and discussion (Beck & McKeown, 2001; O'Connor et al., 1996; O'Connor, 2000). Moreover, neither beginning level of vocabulary nor socioeconomic level depresses children's ability to learn to decode words in the primary grades when instruction has been careful (O'Connor, Fulmer, Harty, & Bell, 2005).

ACTIVITIES TO DEVELOP CHILDREN'S VOCABULARY AND ORAL LANGUAGE

It would be useful for all children to start their schooling with richly developed oral language and knowledge of word meanings so that language and reading can optimally facilitate one another. In its chapter on vocabulary, the National Reading Panel's (2000) report on teaching children to read reviewed 50 studies on particular approaches to teaching children the meanings of words. An analysis of the most effective strategies showed that they all had three features in common: (1) teachers taught children a meaning for a word, rather than asking them to guess; (2) teachers encouraged children to say the word and its meaning several times in appropriate contexts during the instructional sessions; and (3) teachers provided many opportunities to review the word over several days. The next section shows these three features threaded throughout research-based methods to improve children's vocabulary and language.

Expanding the Child's Words

Conversing with children around a shared event, such as during mealtime, taking a walk, or reading a book, can improve their vocabulary over time (Dickinson & Tabors, 2001; Weizman & Snow, 2001). The particular feature of adult–child talk that seems to have the greatest influence is conversation in which the adult describes and explains objects and actions that are of interest to the child and encourages the child to repeat and expand the conversation. Although many of the studies have been conducted with parents and their children (e.g., Bennett, Weigel, & Martin, 2002; Storch & Whitehurst, 2002), similar results have been obtained when preschool and kindergarten teachers engage children in explanatory conversations (e.g., Brabham & Lynch-Brown, 2002; O'Connor et al., 1996). The example below shows how an adult can encourage children to use more, and more complex, language.

Expanding a Child's Language during a Spring Walk in the Neighborhood

ADULT	CHILD
	Ooh. What is it? (*Points to the curled tip of a fiddlehead fern an inch above the earth.*)
It looks like a fern just starting to grow.	A fern.
The ground must be warming up. Yes, the air is still cold, but the ground is warming up. Do you feel it?	It's cold! Brr.
	(*Touches the ground and nods.*) It's warming up.
Do you feel the sun on your back? This plant has been hiding under the ground all winter.	(*Nods.*) It's warming up.
	It was hiding.
Hiding underground so it won't freeze. But now the fern feels that sunshine, just like we do.	Brr. It's freezing.
	I feel the sunshine. I feel it on my coat.
Now the snow is gone, and the sun warms your coat, and the sun warms the ground, and the plants start to grow again.	This is growing? It doesn't look like a fern.
It isn't grown up yet. See—the top is curled up tightly. Let's look again next Saturday and see if it looks more like a fern when it grows a little more.	(*Points to the tip of a daffodil leaf that is just coming up nearby.*) Is this a fern?
Do they look the same to you?	(*Examines each plant.*) This fern is curled up and brown, but this one is green and pointy.
So it must be a different plant, but the sunshine today is helping it grow, too.	(*Begins to notice other plants coming up in the gardens along the street.*)

Both of the procedures that follow incorporate a similar kind of expansion of the child's language and concepts in the instructional routines.

Text Talk

In their work in kindergarten classrooms, Beck and McKeown (2001) found that children with poor vocabularies often provide only one-word responses to teachers' encouragement to enter a conversation. They developed a read-aloud procedure called Text Talk to engage children in discussion of words and story concepts. The two key features of Text Talk are eliciting greater language production from youngsters and directly teaching the meanings of important and unusual words in the stories teachers read to children. In Text Talk, teachers begin by reading a story aloud to children and discussing the content and story concepts with them.

To elicit descriptive language from children, teachers repeat and rephrase each child's first response. By repeating and rephrasing, teachers illustrate how children's thoughts can be elaborated on and expressed grammatically. Imagine this conversation:

CHILD: Monkey say night night.

TEACHER: Yes, the monkeys said good night to their mama.

CHILD: The monkeys said, "Good night, Mama."

TEACHER: Now what do you think those monkeys will do?

CHILD: Jump!

TEACHER: The moneys will jump on the bed?

CHILD: The monkeys will JUMP on the bed!

TEACHER: (*Turns the page.*) Are the monkeys jumping?

CHILD: The monkeys are jumping on the bed! Ooh, look, this monkey dancing.

TEACHER: This monkey is dancing on the bed.

In using Text Talk, teachers also teach children the meanings of new words and concepts. The following example is from the teachers' notes for *A Pocket for Corduroy* (Freeman, 1978):

> In the story, Lisa was reluctant to leave the laundromat without Corduroy. Reluctant means you are not sure you want to do something. Say the word with me: Reluctant.
>
> Someone might be reluctant to eat a food that they never had before, or someone might be reluctant to ride a roller coaster because it looks too scary. Think about something you might be reluctant to do. Start your sentence with "I might be reluctant to _____." After each child responds call on another child to explain the response. For example, if a child says, "I might be reluctant to eat spinach" ask another child, "What does it mean that Mike is reluctant to eat spinach?" (Beck & McKeown, 2001, pp. 16–17)

To incorporate the frequent review of new words that is so important to developing an enriched vocabulary, Beck and McKeown recommend that teachers post a wall chart of new words with tally marks for each time the word is used or cited in a new context. Note how the procedures in Text Talk incorporate all three of the features found to be most effective for teaching vocabulary by the National Reading Panel (2000): teaching a meaning directly, encouraging children to use the word and meaning multiple times, and reviewing new words over several days.

Shared Book Reading (Dialogic Reading)

Many variations of shared book reading have been developed, but perhaps the most researched version is dialogic reading, which was developed by Whitehurst and colleagues (Whitehurst et al., 1988; Whitehurst & Lonigan, 1998). Commonly used in preschool, the simple procedures can also be used at home between parent and child or in kindergarten with groups of children. The cornerstones of dialogic reading include active engagement of children during reading and responding to children's words with more sophisticated language.

In dialogic reading, an adult reads a story to a child, but instead of passively listening, the child is encouraged to actively interpret the text and pictures and to elaborate the story beyond the words on the page. The parent or teacher asks questions along several structural dimensions ("What is he doing here?" "Why do you think he wants to do that?"). Whitehurst recommends that teachers begin by asking "wh-" questions (e.g., what, why, where) and repeating children's responses to elicit more elaboration from the children. He also provides a hierarchy of prompts to prolong conversations with children, including recall ("Do you remember who lives in the woods?"), open-ended questions ("Will he follow that advice?"), and distancing questions ("Has that ever happened to you?").

An example of an adult and child engaged in dialogic reading follows. It is clear from their conversation that the child has heard this story many times, so the adult is prompting the child to retell the story.

DIALOGIC READING WITH *ABIYOYO* BY SEEGER AND HAYS (1986)

ADULT	CHILD
Once upon a time, there was a little boy who played the	
	Ukulele.
Yes, there's the ukulele. Do the grown-ups like that ukulele?	No.
What do they say?	Take that thing out of here!
Yes, take that thing out of here. And here's his father.	And he's a magician.
Uh-huh. What is he doing here?	He has a magic wand, and he goes "Zoop zoop!" and things just appear.
They disappear.	They disappear. Zoop zoop!
And what happens?	They disappear.

That's right, they disappear. (*Turns the page*.) Uh-oh . . .

And she wants to drink the water, but the glass disappears. (*Turns the page*.) And the saw disappears.

Why is that a problem?

The men can't work without the saw. Zoop! No saw.
(*Turns the page*.) Zoop! No chair.

(*Turns the page*.) And what do the people say?

You get out of here. Just get!

Yes, and here's that hard word, look— ostracized. Say that.

Ostracized.

The boy and his father were ostracized. That means they made them live on the edge of town.

All alone?

Away from their neighbors. They were ostracized. Why do you think they were ostracized?

'Cause he plays tricks, and he plays the ukulele.

That's right. (*Turns the page*.) What's happening here?

He tells stories about the giant.

And the giant was called _____.

Abiyoyo!

Tell me about Abiyoyo.

He was tall as a tree, and he could eat people up!

Did the people believe Abiyoyo was real?

No, but he was real . . .

The teacher's questions encourage the child to use the author's language, which is often more advanced than the day-to-day words the child uses to communicate. When the story is read in this interactive fashion several times, children are able to use increasingly sophisticated language and will offer more open-ended comments on their own. The adult can repeat and elaborate on each child's responses and observations, continuing the conversation that contains complex language.

These activities are useful for children during the preschool years (Bus, 2001), and they continue to be useful during the first years of reading acquisition in kindergarten, first, and second grades (Goldenberg, Reese, & Gallimore, 1992) because learning the meanings of words and learning to read them can be mutually facilitative. At least through the early grades in school, an interactive style of reading to children—in which children's questions about words, their meanings, and story events are encouraged—promotes growth in vocabulary more than just reading stories straight through (Brabham & Lynch-Brown, 2002).

SOME CAUTIONS ON THE RESEARCH
ON THE ROLE OF ORAL LANGUAGE IN READING WORDS

Research suggests that the influence of oral language on reading ability depends on which aspects of reading were studied (e.g., decoding, reading comprehension), the age of the participants in the studies (e.g., children in preschool or the primary grades, adults), and the way in which oral language was measured (e.g., receptive or expressive vocabulary, listening comprehension). For students of average intelligence in kindergarten, receptive vocabulary exerts very little influence on children's learning of letters, sounds, phoneme awareness, or decoding (O'Connor, Jenkins, & Slocum, 1995), and this lack of strong influence persists into first grade (O'Connor & Jenkins, 1999; Vellutino & Scanlon, 1987), although the role of receptive vocabulary grows as children progress through school. Poor readers often have vocabulary difficulties (Catts, Fey, Zhang, & Tomblin, 1999; Scarborough, 1990); however, poor vocabulary need not inhibit learning the skills that contribute most to reading words, such as those described in the next few chapters of this book.

Although abundant evidence suggests that children with oral-language difficulties can acquire letter–sound relations and decoding skills, persistent language difficulties that influence vocabulary growth are likely to impede reading comprehension by the middle elementary grades (Nation & Snowling, 1999). Not only are students with language difficulties in preschool prone to continued language difficulties later in school (and life), but these early language problems also increase the likelihood of reading problems (Catts et al., 1999).

This body of research suggests two very important points. First, oral language is important for reading comprehension, and, therefore, parents and preschool teachers should do all they can to increase the opportunities young children have to develop vocabulary and listening comprehension. Second, if children enter school with poorly developed vocabulary, it is not too late. Good teaching and increased opportunities with books and stories can continue to exert a positive influence on language and reading development through the first several years in school. The key notion here is that children can and do learn to read words even if their oral language is impoverished, and as those children are learning to read words, teachers can continue to work on improving their oral language.

CHAPTER 2

Phonemic Awareness

Most children pass through the doorway into reading during the first grade. The timing is as important as the passage; if the door opens late, the child misses months or years of the facilitation that reading provides for nearly all academic and cognitive endeavors in school. Sadder still, for children who read poorly at the end of first grade, the door will likely remain closed (Good, Simmons, & Kame'enui, 2001; Scarborough, 2001).

Lack of phonemic awareness—access to the phonology of language that allows reflection and conscious manipulation of the sounds that make up words—may be the key that has locked the door against children who have difficulty acquiring early reading skills (Stanovich, 1986; Tunmer, Herriman, & Nesdale, 1988). Liberman and Shankweiler (1985) suggested that reading relies on knowledge of the sound structure of spoken and written words, particularly the knowledge that words can be broken into sounds called phonemes and that letters represent phonemes rather than syllables or whole words. The ability to manipulate spoken language by assembling sounds into words, breaking words into sounds, and recognizing sound-based similarities in words helps children to make sense of our alphabetic system of writing words.

Even though oral language begins in early childhood with understanding the meanings of words, for children to progress from speaking and listening to reading and writing, they need to think about a word not only as meaningful, but as a collection of sounds. When children can hear and isolate sounds in spoken words (e.g., be able to say each syllable in *basketball* or to generate a word that rhymes with *turtle*), they are said to have phonological awareness. When they can hear individual speech sounds, or phonemes (e.g., the /f/ sound at the beginning of *fast* or the /sh/ at the end of *fish*), they are said to have phonemic awareness, which influences how well they will learn the sounds of alphabet letters and, eventually, how well they will read and spell words. How do we know that phonemic awareness influences learning to read words? Let's examine the research trail that led to this conclusion.

LINKING PHONEMIC AWARENESS AND READING WORDS

For the last 25 years, the most common method of identifying a reading disability has been to wait and watch until a student experienced significant failure in school. This "wait and see" approach was set in motion by the definition of learning disability, which required a significant discrepancy between a student's cognitive ability (usually measured with an IQ score) and his or her reading ability (usually measured with a standardized, individually administered reading test). This approach to identification was not very useful in kindergarten, where children who are developing typically are not expected to read very much, or even in first grade, where most children are still beginners.

In the 1980s, as they are today, researchers were interested in whether reading skill could be predicted early enough to prevent the years of school failure that often accompanied a late diagnosis of reading disability. Three studies in particular stand out. Share, Jorm, MacLean, and Matthews (1984) used a broad array of measures administered to kindergartners in Australia to predict how well they would read and spell in first grade. Perfetti, Beck, Bell, and Hughes (1987) began their measurement of children early in first grade to predict how well they would read at the end of the year. Juel (1988) tested children in first grade and followed their reading progress through the end of fourth grade. In all of these studies, the children who could blend speech sounds together (for example, could guess the word *fish* when they heard the isolated sounds /f/-/i/-/sh/) or could break a spoken word into its constituent sounds (for example, could say each of the three sounds in the word *sat*) turned out to be better readers. Perfetti et al. and Juel also reported that decoding instruction in first grade was likely to be ineffective unless children could hear the sounds in spoken words. Taken together, these studies found that phonemic awareness was more predictive of reading development than students' IQ or the socioeconomic level of the home. These findings seemed to indicate good news because a child's phonemic awareness could be easier for teachers to change than a child's innate ability or the socioeconomic level of the household.

Although the importance of phonemic awareness to reading development has since been established, the link was initially puzzling because phonemic awareness does not involve print directly. Phonemic awareness is sound play. The child who teases his or her friend with rhyme ("Sally, wally, pally, dally") or who enjoys the alliteration in *Tiny Tommy Tittlemouse* is showing an early level of phonological awareness because he or she hears the sameness of sounds across words. Moreover, few reading curricula for kindergartens and first grades in the 1990s offered activities that could help teachers teach students to hear all of the sounds in one-syllable words. Researchers hesitated to insist that teachers use instructional activities to develop children's phonemic awareness because they were uncertain whether phonemic awareness exerted a causal influence on reading or whether good reading and strong phonemic awareness just happened to go together without a causal influence in either direction. In the next decade, several researchers conducted experiments to determine this influence.

The question at the heart of these experiments has been: Will improving children's phonemic awareness improve their ability to read words? To answer this question, researchers taught nonblenders to blend and nonsegmenters to segment, while carefully monitoring any reading improvement that might occur as a result of this instruction. The first experiments in which kindergarten children were taught to blend and segment spoken words (Bradley & Bryant, 1985; Lundberg, Frost, & Petersen, 1988) showed small advantages in children's reading and spelling achievement over time. When children also learned some of the alphabet letters and their sounds, the effect on reading and spelling strengthened (Ball & Blachman, 1991). The consistent results of these studies and others that followed led to the current recommendation that children receive instruction in phonemic awareness in kindergarten and first grade, unless they already demonstrate the ability to blend and segment speech sounds.

This recommendation leads to an important point. Many students in kindergarten and first grade already possess these skills, which they learned informally through interactions with adults, books, and environmental print. Should all students be taught to blend and segment sounds or only those who cannot do these things unless they are taught to do so? In studies where children with and without these skills were taught together (O'Connor et al., 1996; O'Connor, 2000; Vaughn, 2003), no disadvantages for children with higher skill levels were found. Therefore, current recommendations for reading instruction (National Report Panel, 2000; Snow, Burns, & Griffin, 1998; Stanovich, 2000) include activities to stimulate phonemic awareness in kindergarten and early in first grade for children with and without risk for reading problems later in school.

ACTIVITIES TO DEVELOP PHONEMIC AWARENESS

Beginning kindergartners enter school with varying knowledge of letters, letter sounds, and phonemic awareness that ranges from no knowledge at all to quite a lot. Luckily for teachers, some of the most successful activities to teach phonemic awareness do not require knowledge of letters and their sounds and so can be used in the very first days of school. Moreover, some of the most successful activities are gamelike and easy to use with groups of young children, particularly in kindergartens.

To teach phonemic awareness in first grade, the same activities can be used, but letters should be added from the very beginning of the school year to represent the sounds in words. By integrating phonemic awareness with the letter sounds children have learned, children quickly grasp the alphabetic principle. More about the alphabetic principle and how to make students aware of it can be found in Chapter 3.

The first hurdle that children need to vault is that of deconstructing one-syllable words. Up until the time we ask children to read or spell, they have considered words only as meaningful units. That is, children know what a cat is, and know several words that they can use to label the furry creature (for example, *cat, kitty, Sophie*). Nevertheless, if you ask a young child to tell you the first sound in *cat*, you are as likely to get a response of "Meow" as "/k/." Young children think about words as labels and actions, but rarely do they attend to the speech sounds that make up the words.

To increase the salience of speech sounds, researchers who study articulation and reading (e.g., Calfee, Lindamood & Lindamood, 1973; Torgesen, 2000) have demonstrated the important additive effect that seeing and feeling how words are pronounced in the mouth has on hearing these same sounds in words. Whether the advantage comes from the kinesthetic experience of forming each sound with the lips and tongue or from the visual reinforcement of sounds as children see how each sound looks on the faces of teacher and classmates is open to debate, but focusing on the visual production of sounds in words tends to be more effective than focusing only on listening to the sounds.

Stretched Segmenting

One of the easiest ways to teach children to hear the sounds in words is to show them how to say words very slowly, holding each sound for about 1 second. When we say words in normal speech, the phonemes in the word fly by so quickly that children find it difficult to hear any single speech sound within the word. Stretched segmenting allows children to focus on each phoneme in a word individually.

Choose words of one syllable that begin with sounds that can be stretched out, such as *fin, foot, lamb, make, run*, etc. (words that begin with *a, e, f, i, l, m, n, o, r, s, u, v, w, y*, and *z* can be stretched). Next, model for children how to say these words very slowly by pausing for at least 1 second on the first and second sounds in the word. For example, a teacher might say, "I can say a word really slowly. Listen and watch me: *mmmaaannn*. Do it with me." Encourage children to say the word slowly with you, pausing one second on each sound: "*mmmaaannn*." Repeat the word with the children several times so that all of them join in and feel and see how each sound forms in the mouth.

As children say words slowly, they also benefit from a teacher's hand and body cues. Two effective models that teachers can use to make abstract sounds in words more concrete are handsweeps and finger signals. For a handsweep, the teacher guides the slow pronunciation of a word by stretching the left hand straight out from the center of the body and slowly moving the left hand out to the side as children repeat the stretched word. Using the left hand is important when children face the teacher, because it emphasizes the left-to-right progression of sounds in reading and writing.

Tip: Try out this procedure. If you use your *right* hand, children will see the sounds progressing right to left, in reverse order from how words are printed on a page. If you signal children with your *left* hand, children will see the left-to-right progression you want to reinforce.

The left hand is also appropriate for finger signals in which the teacher raises first the index finger, then the middle finger, and then the ring finger to represent the changing sounds as children say a word slowly. The most natural way to hold the hand up is with the back of the hand facing the teacher. Using the left hand reinforces what the children will see as left-to-right representation of each new sound in a word—just like spelling. Again, if in doubt, try it with each hand with a partner watching to see the effect of each.

Teaching Stretched Segmenting

TEACHER	STUDENTS
First word:	
I can say a word really slowly. Listen and watch me. I'll say *lap* slowly. You could sit in my *lap*. Llllaaaap. Say it with me: llllaaaap. (*Guides the slow pronunciation by raising his left arm toward students and slowly moving his left hand out from his body as he says the phonemes.*)	Llllaaaap.
That was really slow! Let's say *lap* slowly again. Llllaaaap. (*Again visually guides the slow pronunciation of each sound with his left hand as students and teacher say the word slowly together.*)	(*Watch the teacher's hand.*) Llllaaaap.
Now you do it. (*Silently guides the slow pronunciation with his left hand as the group of students stretches each sound in the word.*)	Llllaaaap.
[If students have difficulty, say an incorrect sound, or fail to articulate the /l/ and /a/ long enough to hear the sound, the teacher coarticulates the sound with the students, provides another model ("Listen: Lllaaap. Do it with me: lllaaap."), and reinforces students' attempts ("That was really slow! Great!").]	(*Make an error.*) Lllaaap.

Next word:

Listen to *fish* the slow way. I like to watch fish in the pool: Fffiiishshsh. Do it with me. (*Guides the slow pronunciation by raising his left arm toward students and slowly moving his left hand out from his body as he says the phonemes.*)	Fffiiishshsh.

[Continue with *Sam, mop, nose, run.*]

Stretched Blending

Think about what children need to do when they see a word they do not instantly recognize. They need to identify the letters, generate a sound for each letter, and then blend the sounds together to attempt to pronounce the word. If the word is spelled regularly (for example, *let, man,* and *box,* but not *laugh* and *they,* which have irregular spellings) and they can perform those three steps, they will probably identify the word correctly. Of the three steps, children with reading problems have the most difficulty with the third step, blending the sounds together (Slocum, O'Connor, & Jenkins, 1993). That is why it makes sense to teach children to blend sounds very early in their schooling, as young as kindergarten. Blending can be taught before children know any of the letters or their sounds by teaching it as a picture activity.

Begin by showing children four objects (e.g., pen, chalk, desk, map) or four pictures (e.g., fish, light, sail, book). Tell them the name of each object or picture and ask them to repeat the names. By naming and having children repeat the names, teachers can invite English language learners to join the activity and ensure that all children have the appropriate word in mind as they try to blend the sounds the teacher provides.

Next, mix the order of the pictures and objects and say each name in a stretched fashion. For example, say, "I'm going to name each picture in a funny way. Listen to this: fffiiishshsh. Say it in that funny way with me." (Teacher and children together say the stretched form of *fish.*) Then ask, "Which word was that?" Because children are focusing on only one of four possibilities, and because they have said the word in that stretched fashion and felt the sounds in their mouths, they are likely to identify the correct word. Use two or three sets of objects or pictures each session, so that the total instructional time is about 5–7 minutes.

After several days of practice, teachers can begin to use words without pictures. If children experience difficulty, teachers can return to the stage of representing each word with a picture or object until children can more easily blend the sounds they hear into words. This procedure is shown below.

The teacher shows children the following pictures:

TEACHER	STUDENTS

TEACHER

Let's name these pictures together.
(*Touches the fox.*) Fox.
(*Touches the soap.*) Soap.
(*Touches the sheep.*) Sheep.
(*Touches the van.*) Van.

Perfect! Let's name them again.
(*Touches the pictures in random order once or twice and corrects errors by naming the picture and asking students to repeat the correct name.*)

Now I'm going to say the names of the pictures in a funny way. If you think you know which picture it is, raise your hand.

Vvvaaannn. (*Says the word slowly with about 1 second on each sound in the word.*) Say it with me that funny way. Vvvaaannn.

What was that?

Here's another picture word: fffooox. Say it with me, then raise your hand when you know which picture it is: fffooox.

STUDENTS

(*Repeat.*) Fox.
(*Repeat.*) Soap.
(*Repeat.*) Sheep.
(*Repeat.*) Van.

(*Name pictures as a group as the teacher touches each one.*)

Vvvaaannn. (*Hands go up.*)

Van!

Fffooox. (*Hands go up.*)

What was that?   Fox!

[Continue with *sheep* and *soap*.]

[If students say the wrong picture
name, say, "No, not _____
(child's response)," repeat the word
slowly, ask children to repeat the
stretched form with you, and ask
again.]

Isolating the First Sound

Saying words slowly and blending sounds into recognizable words are both
important steps toward phonemic awareness. Another important step is identifying the first sound in a spoken word. This level of awareness is useful for students
who are trying to write words as well as to read them because without the ability to
pick out a beginning sound (and, of course, to represent that sound with an alphabet letter), children have no way to begin capturing the words they want to write
with printed letters.

Teachers can make use of stretched forms of words to teach students to hear
and say the first sound in words. Begin by asking students to say a word slowly
several times, as in stretched segmenting. On the third or fourth trial, alert the students that you will stop them while they are saying the word: "Now say *fog* slowly,
and I will stop you." As children begin to articulate clearly the stretched first sound
("/fff/"), stop students and ask what sound they made: ("Stop. What sound was
that? Yes, /fff/ is the first sound in *fog*." This technique eliminates wordy explana-
tions, and most students will give a correct response the first time. Provide practice
by repeating the activity with five to eight words each day for several days. When
children can stop on the first sound easily and seldom make errors, ask them to
identify the first sound without stretching the whole word: "*Mitt*. What's the first
sound you hear in *mitt*?"

Not all words can be stretched. Some words begin with consonants that cannot
be stretched (e.g., the consonants *b*, *d*, *t*), so teach children to iterate the first sounds
by saying something like, "I can say *top* in a funny way. Listen to this: t-t-t-top. Say
it with me." Guide students to say the word with the first sound iterated: "Say *top*
in that funny way, and I will stop you." After students have clearly articulated the
first iterated sound ("/t-t-t/"), stop them and ask, "What sound did you say?"
(Students respond, "/T/.") "Yes, /t/ is the first sound in *top*." Use five to eight
words (for example, *boy, cow, dog, goat, hop, talk*) each session for several days, and
then ask students to identify the first sound in a word without first iterating the
first sound: "*Tail*. What's the first sound you hear in *tail*?"

Teaching Students to Say the First Sound in a Word

TEACHER	STUDENTS
For words with stretchable first sounds.	
Let's say *fan* slowly. Fffaaannn. (*Pauses on each sound for 1 full second.*)	Fffaaannn.
Do it again.	Fffaaannn.
Do it again, but this time I'll stop you on the first sound.	/Fff/.
Stop. What sound was that?	/Fff/.
Yes, /fff/ is the first sound in fffan.	
What's the first sound in fffan?	/Fff/.
[Continue with *milk, vote, at.*]	
For words with first sounds that cannot be stretched:	
I'll say *bike* in a funny way: b-b-bike.	
Do it with me: b-b-bike	B-b-bike.
Do it again.	B-b-bike.
Do it again, but this time I'll stop you on the first sound.	/B-b-b/.
Stop. What sound was that?	/B-b/.
Yes, /b/ is the first sound in bike.	
[Continue with *doll, bear, pup.*]	

Isolating the Ending Phoneme

Identifying the first sound in a word is a start toward hearing sounds smaller than syllables; however, by itself, the first sound does not provide the level of phonemic segmentation needed for reading words. In fact, when students cannot proceed beyond hearing the first sound, the only strategies available for reading words are to memorize them or to look at the first sound and guess, which is a very difficult habit to break.

To teach students to locate and identify the last sound in spoken words, begin by asking students to say a word slowly several times. On the third or fourth trial, alert the students that you will stop them while they are saying the word: "Now say *rain* slowly, and I will stop you." (Children say, "/rrraaainnn/.") As children clearly articulate the stretched last sound ("/nnn/"), stop them and ask what sound they made: "Stop. What sound was that? Yes, /nnn/ is the last sound in *rain*." As with first-sound activities, provide practice by repeating the activity with five to eight words each day for several days. When children can stop on the last sound easily and seldom make errors, ask them to identify the last sound without stretching the whole word: "*Mitt.* What's the last sound you hear in *mitt*?"

Teaching Students to Say the Last Sound in Words

TEACHER	STUDENTS
Let's say *ran* slowly. Rrraaannn. (*Pauses on each sound for 1 full second.*)	Rrraaannn.
Do it again.	Rrraaannn.
Do it again, but this time I'll stop you on the last sound.	Rrraaaannn.
Stop. What sound was that?	/Nnn/.
Yes, /n/ is the last sound in rannn.	
What's the last sound in rannn?	/Nnn/.
Let's say *egg* slowly. Eeeg.	Eeeg.
Do it again.	Eeeg.
Do it again, but this time I'll stop you on the last sound.	Eeeg.
Stop. What was the last sound in egg?	/G/.
Yes, /g/ is the last sound in egg.	
What's the last sound in egg?	/G/.

[Continue with *goat, lip, lamb, rock.*]

Isolate the Middle Phoneme

The same procedure can be used to teach students to locate and identify the medial vowel sound in spoken words, which for most students is the most difficult sound in a word to hear (McCandliss, Beck, Sendak, & Perfetti, 2003). Ask students to say a word slowly, but stop them while they are saying the medial sound: "Now say *fin* slowly, and I will stop you." (Children say /"Fffiiinnn/.") As children clearly articulate the stretched middle sound (/iii/), stop them and ask what sound they made: "Stop. What sound was that? Yes, /iii/ is the middle sound in *fin*." As with all phonemic awareness activities, practice will be needed for several days. When children can find the middle sound easily and seldom make errors, ask them to identify the middle sound without stretching the whole word: "*Lake.* What's the middle sound in *lake*?"

In preschool or kindergarten, some children have difficulty with the concepts of first, middle, and last. Teachers may need to teach these terms with visual aids, such as trains (engine, middle cars, caboose), sandwiches (bottom slice, filling, top slice), or three children lining up for recess.

Teaching Students to Find the Middle Sound in Words

TEACHER	STUDENTS
Let's say *mad* slowly. Mmmaaad. (*Pauses on each sound for 1 full second.*)	Mmmaaad.
Do it again.	Mmmaaad.
Do it again, but this time I'll stop you on the middle sound in *mad*.	Mmmaaa.
Stop. What sound was that?	/Aaa/.
Yes, /a/ is the middle sound in maaad.	
What's the middle sound in maaad?	/Aaa/.

[If students make errors, the teacher says the word slowly again, and invites children to say it with her. The teacher can provide a visual aid by sweeping her left hand across her body or by touching the table top with her left hand as each sound in the word is stretched. Be sure to move the hand in the direction that sounds occur from the students' view (e.g., backward from the teacher's view).]

Listen again—/mmm/ (*touches the table*) /aaa/ (*touches the table to the left*) /d/ (*touches farther left*).

Do it with me:

| /Mmm/ (*touches the table*) /aaa/ (*touches the table to the left*) / d/ (*touches farther left*). | Mmmaaad. |
| Do it again, and I'll stop you on the middle sound. | Mmmaaa. |

Yes, /a/ is the middle sound in maaad.

[Continue with *rope, vase, book.*]

Segmenting Words into All of Their Phonemes

Hearing sounds in particular places in words (first, middle, or last sound) is an important phonemic awareness skill, but to read and spell, children need to learn to say all of the phonemes in short words in sequence. Saying all of the sounds in order is called phonemic segmentation, and this skill is now considered an important target for kindergarten instruction.

Some children appreciate a visual aid to represent the sounds they hear when they begin to segment words beyond the first sound. One such aid was introduced by Elkonin (1973). It provides a connected square and rectangle so that students can touch the square as they identify the first sound and touch the rectangle as they say the rest of the word (e.g., d-uck or S-am).

This level of segmenting, called onset-rime segmentation (the onset is the first consonant or consonant cluster; the rime is the part that begins with the vowel) can help students move from the relatively easy first-sound identification activity to the relatively difficult identification of all sounds in words in sequence. Researchers have found that modeling this level of segmenting for students is easier than trying to explain it with complicated language (Slocum et al., 1993).

Teachers say something like, "I can say a word in two parts. Listen to me. (Teachers show children the boxes.) /S/-at. Say it with me." Teachers encourage students to repeat the parts as they model touching the square for the first sound (/s/) and the longer rectangle for the rime (/at/). Repeat the segmented word several times until students consistently provide the parts correctly. As students learn the onset-rime level of segmenting, teachers can laminate these visual models so that students touch their own boxes as they segment words. As children learn letters and their sounds, they can move a letter tile into the first square to represent the first sound or write the letter that makes the sound with an erasable marker, which is an activity in the next chapter.

Most children who become good readers can segment one-syllable words into all of their constituent sounds by mid-kindergarten and certainly early in first grade (Good et al., 2001; O'Connor, Fulmer, et al., 2005). Words that begin with consonant blends are exceptions to this timetable because they are the most difficult to separate, and, in fact, many children cannot separate the /c/ sound from the /l/ sound in *clock* until after they can read the word.

Teachers can signal the transition from onset-rime to complete segmentation by modeling ("I can say *all* the sounds in *Pat*. Listen to me."), by shifting to a three-finger signal (/p/-/a/-/t/) with one finger for each sound, or by shifting to a three-square form to represent three sounds, as shown below.

Teaching Students to Segment Words into Three Phonemes

Show children the three-square form below:

<small>TEACHER</small>	<small>STUDENTS</small>

<small>TEACHER</small>

Let's say all the sounds in *Pam*. Watch me. *(Touches the first box.)* /P/. *(Touches the middle box.)* /A/. *(Touches the last box.)* /M/.

Watch me again.

(Touches each box as the phoneme is pronounced.) /P/ - /a/ - /m/.

Do it with me. *(Touches each box in sequence as he and the students say the three sounds together.)* /P/ - /a/ - /m/.

<small>STUDENTS</small> /P/ - /a/ - /m/.

Now you say the sounds.

(Touches each box in sequence as the students say the three sounds.) /P/ - /a/ - /m/.

Let's say all the sounds in *like*. Watch me.

(Touches the first box.) /L/. *(Touches the middle box.)* /I/. *(Touches the last box.)* /K/.

Do it with me. *(Touches each box in sequence as he and the students say the three sounds together.)* /L/ - /i/ - /k/.   /L/ - /i/ - /k/.

Now you say the sounds.

(Touches each box in sequence as the students say the three sounds.)   /L/ - /i/ - /k/.

[Continue with *mutt* and *cat*.]

As the children gain confidence saying all the sounds in short words, they also enjoy having their own three-square form to touch as they say each sound. I have found that touching each square or pushing a bean or a disk into each square to represent the sound as they say it helps some children to stay focused on the task at hand.

When teachers integrate three-phoneme segmentation with representing each sound with a letter, they also encourage students to apprehend the alphabetic principle, which is the topic of the next chapter. Other activities to teach phonemic awareness to students in kindergarten and first grade can be found in the collections by O'Connor, Notari-Syverson, and Vadasy (2005), Blachman, Ball, Black, and Tangel (2000), and Adams, Foorman, Lundberg, and Beeler (1997). Information on these resources can be found in Appendix A. Table 2.1 shows a sample time frame for teaching phomemic awareness skills in kindergarten.

TABLE 2.1. Sequence and Time Goals for Phonemic Awareness Skills and the Alphabetic Principle in Kindergarten*

Task	Aim for:	By:
Stretched segmenting	Slow pronunciation that pauses on each speech sound of two- and three-phoneme words that begin with a vowel or single consonant	November
Stretched blending	Correct selection of words represented by pictures that were not used during instruction	November
Identifying the first sound	Nine correct in 10 words that begin with a single consonant	December
Identifying the last sound	Nine correct in 10 words that end with a single consonant	February
Identifying the medial vowel	Eight correct in 10 words	March
Segmenting all sounds	Thirty or more correct segments in 1 minute	April
Combining segmenting with letters (see Chapter 3, "Integrating Phoneme Awareness with Letter Sounds" and "Phoneme Identity")	Eight of 10 correctly spelled (with letter tiles) two- and three-letter words with regular spellings and short (single letter) vowel sounds	May

Note. This timing assumes a 9-month school year that begins in September and runs through June. For year-round schools, count months in kindergarten (e.g., January = Month 5).

A WORD ABOUT CHILDREN LEARNING ENGLISH AS A SECOND LANGUAGE

Research in other languages that rely on a written alphabet, such as Spanish, German, and most European languages, has found a similar facilitative relationship between phonemic awareness and reading words to that found in English. By choosing activities that use pictures to represent words, teachers can help English language learners to learn new vocabulary alongside awareness of the speech sounds in English that constitute the words. All students benefit from naming the words that the pictures represent because it helps them focus on the instruction. Practicing the words before the activity begins also invites children who are English language learners to participate.

ASSESSING PHONEMIC AWARENESS

Given the importance of phonemic awareness for reading words, it makes sense to figure out what students understand about blending and segmenting the sounds in spoken words. Several instruments can help teachers assess students' knowledge in these areas, and good measures are readily available, such as Dynamic Indicators of Basic Early Literacy Skills (DIBELS; Good, Kaminski, Smith, Laimon, & Dill, 2001), the Comprehensive Test of Phonological Processing (CTOPP; Wagner, Torgeson, & Rashotte, 1999), the Texas Primary Reading Inventory (TPRI; Center for Academic Reading Skills, 1999), and the Yopp-Singer Test of Phoneme Segmentation (Yopp, 1988). In recent studies that have used these measures for instructional recommendations (Good et al., 2001; O'Connor et al., 2005; Simmons, Kuykendall, King, Cornachione, & Kame'enui, 2000), researchers have been working to establish optimal levels of phonemic awareness for students at particular grade levels.

For the purpose of stimulating decoding and word recognition, studies converge on the recommendation that students learn to identify the first sound in words midway through kindergarten. That provides time in the remainder of kindergarten for students to work toward identifying all of the sounds in one-syllable, three-phoneme words. Some studies have also suggested that not only should students be able to identify all phonemes in short words by the beginning of first grade, but they should be able to do so effortlessly (Good et al., 2001). Effortlessly means that students should be able to provide all sounds in a list of 10 single-syllable words in about a minute. That rate is not lightning fast; however, no evidence to date exists to suggest that students who can segment at even faster rates are more efficient or accurate in reading words later on in school.

It is also important to realize that segmenting words into individual phonemes may be stage-limited in terms of its role in supporting the development of reading. That is, students need to be able to segment in order to decode words that are unfamiliar, but once they can do so easily, they move into more varied strategies for reading words that include using highly regular word patterns and spellings. When we measure segmenting after students have passed into these flexible strategies, such as those discussed in Chapters 5–7, they appear to regress in segmenting skill because they no longer need to decode words letter by letter, which is the level of reading that segmentation appears to facilitate.

This relationship can be seen in graphs from O'Connor and colleagues (1996) and Vadasy (2001), which demonstrate the way in which segmentation facilitates the beginnings of word reading. For the beginning levels of reading and spelling, improvement in blending and segmenting appears to be linked directly to how well children read and spell. But beyond a score of 28 or so (meaning that children can segment most sounds in 10 three-phoneme words fairly easily), the relationship breaks down. This relationship suggests that if we can raise most children to this level of segmenting (i.e., to say all of the sounds in 10 one-syllable words in 1 minute), it is probably good enough and time to move on to measuring more advanced reading skills. After students can read words by chunking two or more phonemes together, as when they use the *-ight* pattern to read *bright*, measuring segmentation may generate the wrong impression that students can only segment at the level of onset and rime when they have simply become more efficient at reading words.

Teachers can generate a measure of segmentation easily to capture how well their students hear these speech sounds in spoken words:

- Make a list of 12 one-syllable words. Check that *none* of these words begin with consonant clusters, such as *clock, stop, black, street*, etc.
- Use the first two words to demonstrate what you want students to do. "I can say all the sounds in *duck*. Watch me [*tap the table for each sound*]: /d/ - /u/ - /ck/. Can you do that?"
- For the two practice words give students the opportunity to say words in segments after your model.
- Start the test with the remaining 10 words: "What sounds do you hear in *fog*?"
- If students cannot segment any of the first several words, discontinue the test, identify activities to use to teach phonemic awareness over the next few weeks, and test again later.

For students who can provide most of the phonemes in the list of words, use a stopwatch the next time to see if they can say all of the sounds in 10 words within a minute. If they can, they are ready for the activities in Chapters 3 and 4. Sample forms for this type of informal assessment of segmenting can be found in the measurement chapter of *Ladders to Literacy* (O'Connor, Notari-Syverson, et al., 2005), which includes a large collection of effective phonemic awareness, print awareness, and oral-language activities for kindergarten teachers and students. A sample checklist of 12 words can be found in Appendix B of this text. Remember that teachers should use several different lists so that students think about the sounds in the words and do not memorize the answers.

CHAPTER 3

The Alphabetic Principle

Phonemic awareness is an important instructional goal in kindergarten, but by itself, it provides insufficient information for reading words. Without knowledge of letters and sounds, children will be unable to turn the print on the page into spoken words. Moreover, even with knowledge of letter sounds *and* phoneme awareness, some children will still have difficulty reading words. Researchers have identified another understanding crucial to learning to read words: an understanding of the alphabetic principle, in which phonemic awareness and knowledge of letter–sound correspondences come together in the practical application of reading. The alphabetic principle can be understood in this way: Any word that we say can be broken into speech sounds. Any speech sound can be represented with a letter or collection of letters from the alphabet. When children understand the ways in which letters capture speech sounds, they have knowledge of the alphabetic principle, which is the foundation for all reading and spelling in alphabetic languages.

EVIDENCE THAT LINKS THE ALPHABETIC PRINCIPLE TO READING WORDS

We saw the powerful advantages to teaching phonemic awareness to kindergarteners and first graders in the last chapter. In experiments, when alphabet letters were added to instruction in blending and segmenting speech sounds (Byrne & Fielding-Barnsley, 1991; Tangel & Blachman, 1992; O'Connor & Jenkins, 1995), a dramatic improvement occurred in students' ability to read words. Let's examine some of the studies in which the alphabetic principle was taught to young children.

Tangel and Blachman (1992) taught children who were not yet reading words to segment spoken words with the three-square form shown in Chapter 2. They also taught children the common sound for eight alphabet letters and how to represent each segment in a spoken word with one of the letter sounds they had learned. Children improved not only in spelling, which was the focus of their study, but also in their ability to read words.

The spelling intervention used by Tangel and Blachman provided children with a very clear demonstration of the alphabetic principle. Their work and that of others showed that for prereaders, the alphabetic principle does not necessarily come naturally. Instruction in how to combine knowledge of phonemes with knowledge of letter sounds made it much more likely that children would be able to use what they knew to decode a word.

Research on the role of the alphabetic principle in reading words began with studying young children who were prereaders, but with average or high cognitive levels. O'Connor and Jenkins (1995) worked with students in a special education kindergarten who were learning to read with a structured phonics approach. They matched pairs of children by their reading pretest scores and then randomly assigned children to extra practice reading the words from their daily reading program or manipulating letter tiles to spell the same words. Although children in the two treatments did not differ in segmenting or reading ability prior to the treatment, children who were given the spelling practice made the strongest gains in reading, even though their matched controls received as many practice trials reading the words as the spellers received spelling them. O'Connor and Jenkins concluded that spelling the words improved students' understanding of the alphabetic principle. Students learned that changing just one letter in a word altered its identity.

In a similar study with older students, McCandliss and colleagues (2003) found that poor readers in second and third grade who spelled words with Isabel Beck's word building technique (Beck & Hamilton, 2000) began to attend to the medial letters and sounds in words, whereas the control students made many more errors related to medial vowels. In all three studies described above, moving letter tiles to represent the phonemes children heard in words helped them learn to read the words more accurately than children in control conditions. All three studies focused on clear demonstrations of the alphabetic principle.

These studies are important because we often assume that children understand the function of letters in the words they read and spell. Connie Juel (1988) measured children's reading and spelling skills over a 4-year period (first through fourth grades) and found that fourth graders with difficulty reading words had a level of decoding ability that was similar to the first graders who were good readers. Combined with the findings of other studies of good and poor older and younger readers (e.g., Rack, Snowling, & Olson, 1992; Vellutino & Scanlon, 1987), collective evidence suggests that good readers understand the alphabetic principle very early on—generally before the end of first grade. Older poor readers may take years to reach that understanding, and by the time they do understand it, they have missed the opportunity to make use of the alphabetic principle to learn the simple word forms on which further reading development depends.

ACTIVITIES TO DEVELOP AWARENESS OF THE ALPHABETIC PRINCIPLE

Since the alphabetic principle adds measurably to students' growth in reading words, it makes sense to begin to introduce this notion as soon as children have enough phonemic awareness and letter knowledge to begin to link the two. For kindergartners, knowing only four to eight letters and sounds may be enough to begin using those letter sounds in first-sound and last-sound activities. For an explanation of specific teaching routines for letters and sounds, see Chapter 4.

Integrating Phoneme Awareness with Letter Sounds

The onset-rime activity from Chapter 2 is a good place to start to teach the alphabetic principle. Provide children with a small set of letters on laminated cards (for example, *a*, *m*, *d*, *s*), along with the two-box onset-rime grid. When children can break a spoken word into its onset and rime (/d/ - /og/), ask children, "What's the first sound in *dog*?" (Children respond, "/D/.") "Do you know a letter that makes that sound?" (Children respond, "D."] "Put *d* in the first box." In this way, children begin to understand that not only does *dog* begin with the sound /d/, but that the sound can be represented with a letter they have learned to identify. This procedure is shown below.

Teaching Onset-Rime Segmenting with the First Letter

The teacher shows children the onset-rime box and letter tiles, as below:

f p m l

Teacher	Students
Let's say some words in two parts. *Mop.* (*Touches the first square, then the rectangle as students segment the word.*)	/M/ - /op/.
Say *fast* in two parts.	/F/ - /ast/.
Pin.	/P/ - /in/.
Late.	/L/ - /ate/.
Mop.	/M/ - /op/.
(*Touches the first box.*) What's the first sound in *mop*?	/M/.
Do you know a letter that makes that sound?	M.
Yes! Put *m* in the first box.	(*A student moves the* m *tile into the first box.*)
Perfect. Say the parts in *mop*.	(*The student touches the* m.) /M/-/op/. (*The student touches the rectangle.*)
That's right. Say the parts in *fast*.	/F/ - /ast/.
First sound? (*Touches the first box.*)	/F/.
Do you know a letter that makes that sound?	F
Yes! Put *f* in the first box.	(*A student moves the* f *tile into the first box.*)
That's right. Say the parts in *fast*.	(*The student touches the* f.) /F/ - /ast/. (*The student touches the rectangle.*)

[Continue with *pin* and *late*. If students have difficulty with onset-rime segmenting, spend a few sessions teaching this level of segmenting (see Chapter 2) and then reintroduce the activity. If students have difficulty selecting a letter to represent the first sound, spend a few sessions practicing the difficult letter–sound pairings using the cumulative introduction of letters from Chapter 4.]

Phoneme Identity

Using a letter to represent a first sound is a good way to begin to teach the alphabetic principle because the first sound is the easiest sound for children to hear in words. As children's phonemic awareness becomes more sophisticated, other sounds in words can be represented with the letters teachers have taught. Kindergarten curricula have long included first-sound pairings with alphabet letters. Consider the alphabet cards that teachers place around the classroom walls as children learn letters. These cards often show an animal or object that can help cue children to recall a sound the letter often represents at the beginning of a word. For example, *b* is taught, and the letter *b* (with a ball, a bat, a boy, or a box) goes up on the wall. Useful as these cards may be, children need to recognize that the *b* sound at the beginning of *box* is represented by *b* again at the end of *cob* or *fib*. The notion that a letter sound can appear in several positions in words is important because it encourages children to attend to all sounds in words as they learn phonemic awareness and to all letters in words as they learn to decode and read. Therefore, as children learn to recognize the last sound in words and to segment words into three or four phonemes, the letter sounds children have learned can be incorporated into activities. The activity below to teach phoneme identity can be used after students have learned to segment spoken words reliably and to pair each letter in the activity with its sound.

Teaching Phoneme Identity

The teacher shows children the three-square box and letter tiles, as below:

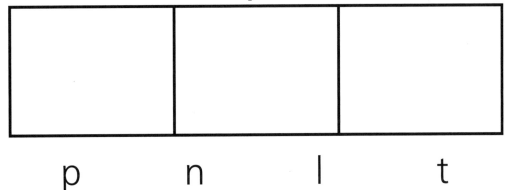

TEACHER	STUDENTS
Touch the squares and say all the sounds in *nap*.	/N/ - /a/ - /p/.
Which letter says /n/?	N!
Good! Put the *n* where it goes in the word.	(*A child puts the* n *in the first box.*)
That's right. Here's another word. *Tin.* Say that word.	*Tin.*
Where does the *n* go now?	/T/ - /i/ - /n/. At the end. (*The child moves the* n *into the last box.*)

Man. Where does the *n* go now?	/M/ - /a/ - /n/. Still at the end.
Touch the squares and say all the sounds in *doll*.	/D/ - /o/ - /l/.
Yes. What's the last sound?	/L/. (*The child finds the* l, *touches the boxes, and rehearses the segments to figure out where to put the* l, *then puts it in the last box.*)
That's where it goes. Where does the *l* go in this word? *Late.*	(*The child touches the boxes and segments* late, *then moves the* l *into the first box.*)

[Continue with *tan, fit, lip,* and *puck,* and end with *pop* to show how a sound can be used twice in a word. If children have difficulty with auditory segmenting of the word, stop this activity and spend several sessions on segmenting (see Chapter 2). If children have difficulty selecting the correct letters, spend a few sessions practicing the difficult letter–sound pairings using the cumulative introduction of letters from Chapter 4.]

WHAT ABOUT INVENTED SPELLING?

When young children are encouraged to label their drawings or generate other written responses, they often lack knowledge of correct spellings for the words they want to capture in print. Nevertheless, attempting spellings for words can help them apprehend the alphabetic principle. Teachers can encourage children to write using what they know and understand about print and sounds in language by suggesting that they say words slowly and listen to the sounds in the word and then try to find letters that could represent the sounds they hear. The experience of inventing spelling differs from segment-to-spell, in which words are deliberately selected because they are composed of letter sounds children have already learned thoroughly. Invented spelling requires children to devote conscious attention to how they might represent the sounds in words logically, even when they have not been taught particular spoken and written word pairings. The logic children use to invent spellings for words is an internal and temporary logic, which can be replaced over time as children become more aware of the letter–sound possibilities in their language.

Many researchers have studied invented spelling. Read (1971), Beers and Henderson (1977), and Clarke (1988) all found that children who invent spellings for words in their labels and messages write more than children who are required to spell words correctly. Shanahan (1980) suggested that children who consciously reflect on the spellings of words may have an advantage in reading. Ehri and Wilce (1985) found that children who were provided with logical, though incorrect, spellings for words (msk for *mask*) learned to read words more accurately in the early stages. The experimental work of Tangel and Blachman (1992) and O'Connor and Jenkins (1995) established the connection between spelling attempts and improvements in reading words.

What about Children Who Won't Try Invented Spelling?

Think about what children need to do when they want to write a word they do not know how to spell. When we watch children try to spell, we often see them looking into space and mouthing the word's pronunciation in an attempt to get started. In that mouthing, children are trying to generate a first sound so that they can write a letter for that sound on paper; then they try to find other sounds that they can represent with letters. In other words, they are trying to segment the word they want to write into its constituent sounds.

If children cannot hear isolated sounds within the word, which is a common problem for young children, especially with words of just one syllable, they simply cannot get started. Instead of a string of likely letters, we see loop-de-loop scribbles as an attempt to write words. In this prealphabetic stage of reading and writing (Ehri, 1995), children have no sound or letter cues to help them generate an invented spelling for a word. To help children grow beyond this stage, teachers need to encourage children to begin to hear the sounds in the word they want to write—children need to learn to segment words. Teachers can help by encouraging children to say words slowly so that the speech sounds in the word become easier to hear. From there, teachers can teach children to isolate the first sound, the last sound, and eventually all of the sounds in short words (see Chapter 2 for teaching strategies). Once children hear the phonemes in words, they can begin to link the letter sounds they are learning to the sounds they hear in words, and invented spelling begins.

SEGMENT-TO-SPELL

Perhaps the most powerful demonstration of the alphabetic principle is during activities where children segment words into all of their constituent sounds, represent each sound with a letter of the alphabet, and then read the word back. In other words, the most powerful way to demonstrate the alphabetic principle is by showing children how to spell simple words, which is precisely what researchers did in the experiments described earlier.

Segment-to-spell differs from traditional spelling in three dimensions. First, students are asked to identify consciously each sound within the word (segment).

Next, as they spell the word, they use their knowledge of segmenting and alphabet letters to generate a spelling, rather than using memorization techniques. Last, teachers have students examine the word that they have spelled, produce a sound for each letter in the word, and blend those sounds back together to regenerate the spoken word with which they started. Segment-to-spell captures all of the dimensions of decoding, along with the kinesthetic experience of moving letters or tiles, which focuses students' attention on the task at hand.

Begin teaching segment-to-spell after students in the instructional group have learned to segment spoken words with two, three, or four phonemes. Choose a short list of words (three or four, as a start) that consist only of letters that have been taught, with no silent letters or vowel combinations that are unusual. For example, suppose students have learned the letters and sounds for *a, m, s, t, i, d,* and *f*. The teacher might decide to use *fat, fit,* and *sad* on the first day. Provide each student in the group with letter tiles or cards for *a, s, t, i, d,* and *f,* and the three-box segmenting card.

Say, "Tell me the sounds you hear in *fat*." (Children say, "/F/ - /a/ - /t/.) If students in the group have difficulty providing the sounds, spend a few sessions providing directed opportunities to segment, such as those in the last chapter. If only one or two students have difficulty segmenting all sounds in *fat*, say, "Say *fat* with me very slowly." (Children say, "Fffaaat.") "Now you say *fat* slowly. (Children: "Ffffaaat.") Now tell me the sounds you hear in *fat*."

"What's the first sound in *fat*? (Children say, "Fff.") "Do you know a letter that makes that sound?" (Children: "F.") Put the *f* in the first box. Now tell me all the sounds in *fat*. (Children: "Fffaaat.") "What's the middle sound in *fat*?" (Children: "Aaa.") "Do you know a letter that makes that sound?" (Children: "A.") "Put the *a* in the middle box. Sound out what you have so far." (Children touch under the *f* and *a* and blend, "/Fffaaa—/.") "What's the last sound in *fat*?" (Children: "/T/.") "Do you know a letter that makes /t/?" (Children: "T.") "Put the *t* in the last box. Now let's sound out what you made." (Students sound out /fffaaat/.) "What word did you make?" (Children: "Fat.") "Sound out the word you made." Have children return the letters to their own collection and use the same teaching technique for fit and *sad*.

In this activity, it is important to consciously link spelling with reading by asking students to read back the word they have spelled. In our studies (for example, O'Connor & Padeliadu, 2000) and in our classrooms, we have known many children who can segment and generate a plausible spelling for a word but who cannot read back the words they spell. When we include blending and segmenting in the same instructional sessions, children learn both more rapidly and have less difficulty decoding (the topic of Chapter 4).

What about Children Who Can't Completely Segment Spoken Words?

Instructional strategies like segment-to-spell are meant for children who can already segment spoken words. Teachers can begin to teach the alphabetic principle less formally by integrating a little letter–sound and segmenting experience with the books they routinely read to students. The books for this activity do not need to be "decodable books," in the sense that most words in the book are simple, short, and regularly spelled. All books have some words that are decodable. Take, for example, the traditional poem "Over in the Meadow":

> Over in the meadow in the sand in the sun,
> Lived an old mother turtle and her little turtle one.
> "Bask," said the mother.
> "I bask," said the one.
> So she basked and was glad in the sand in the sun.

Many words in the poem would be difficult for a beginner to spell. Words such as *meadow* and *lived* have unusual spellings, and even *one* is an irregularly spelled word, even although it is important and occurs frequently in books for young children. On the other hand, words like *sun, sand, in, glad,* and *bask* can be sounded out and spelled accurately by children who can segment and who know the sounds for the letters that make up the word. Teachers can select two or three decodable words from any book they plan to read to a group of children and demonstrate the alphabetic principle by combining opportunities for children to blend auditory sounds, to segment the sounds in the selected word, to represent one or more sounds in the word with letters, to find the word on the page of the book, and to read it. Here is an example.

"I have a mystery word today. See if you can guess my word. /S/ - /u/ - /n/. Do it with me." (Children say, "/S/ - /u/ - /n/.") "What word is that?" (Children: "*Sun.*") "What sounds do you hear in *sun*?" (Children: "/S/ - /u/ - /n/.") "Yes, and what word is that?" (Children: "*Sun.*") "Yes. What's the first sound in *sun*?" (Children: "/S/.") "Do you know a letter that makes that sound?" (Children: "S.") "The teacher writes *s* on the board or a flipchart or moves an *s* tile into the children's work space and says, "Here's /s/. What's the next sound in *sun*?" (Children: "/U/.") "What letter makes /U/?" (Children: "U.") The teacher writes *u* on the board or moves a u tile into the children's work space, and says "What's the last sound in *sun*?" (Children: "/N/.") "So what letter?" (Children: "N.") The teacher completes the spelling of the word and says, "Now let's sound this word out." The teacher touches under each letter and guides children in sounding out the word. "What word did we spell?" (Children: "*Sun.*") "Here's the poem I'll read to you today. Can you find the word *sun* on the page? How do you know that word is *sun*?" The teacher then reads the poem to the children.

By linking all of these activities—blending, segmenting, letter–sound corre-spondences, and blending back the letter sounds in a printed word—the teacher models the alphabetic principle for children. This guided process demonstrates how printed words are generated from sounds to spellings, which provides a model for the alphabetic principle. When this process is used repeatedly, children have a model for generating a spelling for a word they want to write.

Fill in the Blanks

For children who are even more reluctant to write words, consider using pages with the whole class in which children need to write very little and only words that they have confidence in writing. The easiest "fill in" we have found is one in which children only need to know how to write their name to be successful (O'Connor, Notari-Syverson, et al., 2005).

"I begin with _____," said _____.

The teacher has typed this sentence in very large print, leaving plenty of space on the page, and has a copy for every child, plus four or five extra copies to show students how to complete their page. The teacher reads the sentence while pointing to each word and then chooses one student in the class and asks the class to say the name of the student. The teacher prints that child's name after *said* on the page. Next, the teacher points to the child's printed name and asks the class to identify the first letter. The teacher prints that letter after *with* and then reads the completed sentence aloud, again pointing to each word as it is read. After this modeled read-ing, the class can read the sentence aloud with the teacher.

The teacher repeats this activity with a few more students and is careful to include some of the students who are most likely to need assistance. When most children understand exactly how to fill in their sentence, they can take their own copies to their work areas to complete independently. Will the students all finish at the same time? Certainly not, but that is why so much blank space on the page is provided, so that students can draw themselves as other students finish.

When all students are finished with their sentences or the following day, teach-ers can guide students to read all of their classmates' sentences by placing the stack of papers on a flipchart or chalkboard tray and pointing to each word as students read in chorus. Because most students learn to read each others' names early in the school year, teachers can use this activity in mid-kindergarten or September of first grade to demonstrate the alphabetic principle and to get students started with writ-ing. Not all children will learn to read all of the words in the sentence out of context with this activity, but the repetition will be sufficient for some students to learn the words as sight words and for all students to learn that the words on the page, which do not vary, are the same words they are reading as they go from one page to another. More examples for integrating phonemic awareness with letters and their sounds can be found in *Ladders to Literacy* (O'Connor, Nortari-Syverson, et al., 2005), which is listed among the resources in Appendix A.

These activities may seem very easy and obvious. Don't all children understand that writing captures speech? Don't all children understand that the way writing captures speech is first to break each spoken word into sounds and then to represent each sound with a letter or letters from the alphabet? Unfortunately, not all children do understand the alphabetic principle in kindergarten, first grade, or even second grade, where it will do them the most good as they learn to read and write. Rather, students with reading disabilities may continue for several years in school without understanding this most fundamental principle (Juel, 1988). For example, we have measured the segmenting and alphabetic understandings of fourth and fifth graders with reading difficulties (O'Connor et al., 2002), and found (as did Juel) levels typical of first graders. The good news is that older students who spend a few minutes a day doing segment-to-spell or word building quickly acquire the alphabetic principle, and, as a result, their ability to read words improves (McCandliss et al., 2003; O'Connor et al., 2002). In the words of a bright fourth grader diagnosed with a reading disability who spent 6 months in a structured program designed to teach the alphabetic principle and decoding, "Why didn't somebody show me how to do this in first grade? I could have learned it way back then!" Our goal for this book is to provide tools for teachers so that they can, indeed, teach all children to learn the foundational skills needed for reading words early in students' reading careers.

CHAPTER 4

Beginning to Decode

When students understand how reading and writing work reciprocally to turn speech into printed words and printed words back into speech (the alphabetic principle), they are ready to begin to learn how to decode the words they see. Decoding does not come naturally for many children. Rather, it takes careful instruction from teachers and sincere effort from students to reach the point of decoding independently.

The collection of these next chapters describes the strategies for teaching students to read simple words, words with letter patterns, words that cannot be sounded out, and multisyllabic words, along with the research that supports each collection of strategies. First, a word about phonics.

It is impossible to teach all of the letter–sound correspondences that students will need to be able to sound out unknown words. Nevertheless, phonics instruction is useful because it prompts students to look for the relationship between the letters in a printed word and the sounds they hear when saying the word. As students link speech sounds with letters and letter patterns during phonemic awareness activities that are integrated with letter sounds and during attempts to spell, these relationships become clearer. Teachers can jumpstart students' grounding for decoding by teaching the most common letter sounds and letter patterns in words.

PHONICS AND PHONEMIC AWARENESS

Many teachers are confused between the terms "phonics" and "phonemic aware-ness." If we teach children to segment a word, isn't that a lot like phonics? If we teach children to sound out a word by blending each letter sound in a word, isn't that phonemic awareness? Yes . . . and no.

Let's begin with "no." Strictly speaking, phonemic awareness does not involve printed words or even letters. Phonemic awareness is the sound play around spo-ken words that includes isolating speech sounds ("What's the last sound in *flat?*") and manipulating sounds in spoken words ("Say *cup*. Now say *cup*, but don't say /k/"). As soon as we introduce letters and the sounds they represent in words, we are teaching phonics. But research around the role of phonics in reading (e.g., Perfetti, Beck, Bell, & Hughes, 1987) suggests that students cannot make much sense of phonics instruction (learning the sounds of alphabet letters) unless they already have phonemic awareness. When we use instructional activities that enable children to understand the alphabetic principle, such as segment-to-spell (see Chapter 3), we combine phonemic awareness ("Tell me the sounds you hear.") and phonics ("Do you know a letter that makes that sound?") in each instructional session. In these activities, phonics and phonemic awareness are so intertwined that it is difficult to tell the difference, which is how we get to "yes."

Decoding words depends on students' level of skill in at least three areas. Stu-dents need to be able to generate a sound for each letter in the word, to blend speech sounds together, and to segment the pronunciation they generate back into its constituent sounds to check their decoding. In other words, students need all of the skills in the last two chapters, along with knowledge of the sounds letters usu-ally make in short words. As they read several words in a phrase or sentence, they also need the oral-language skills introduced in Chapter 1. No wonder some chil-dren have difficulty learning to read even simple words!

INSTRUCTIONAL PRINCIPLES FOR TEACHING LETTER SOUNDS

The heart of phonics instruction is teaching the basic sounds of the alphabet letters systematically. Although no single phonics program has yet been found that is superior to all others, the advantages for systematic phonics instruction are consis-tently reported. (See Adams, 1990; Chall, 1967, 1996; National Reading Panel, 2000 for reviews of the phonics research. See Carnine, 1977; Foorman, Francis, Fletcher, Schatschneider, & Mehta, 1998; Juel & Minden-Cupp, 2000, for instructional com-parisons and effects.) Systematic phonics instruction begins early and continues until students know the single letters and combinations that make up the pho-nemes in English (or in another alphabetically represented language).

Phonics programs differ in how they introduce letters and sounds, the pacing of introduction, the choice of long or short vowel sounds, the size of the unit (single letters or letter-group patterns and word families), involvement of spelling, and many other dimensions. The recommendations that follow are based on the current evidence, with citations for the research that supports particular approaches.

Avoid Alphabetical Order

Which letters do students confuse the most often? *B* and *d*? *E* and *i*? Carnine, Silbert, and Kame'enui (1997) recommend separating the letters teachers know will be confusing by several instructional weeks. By waiting until students know one letter–sound pairing thoroughly (for example, the shape of *d* and its sound, /d/), students will have less difficulty with the confusable letter (the shape of *b* and its sound, /b/).

Consider the 5-year-old child, and what she knows about her world. The cat walks into a room, and she calls it a cat. The cat leaves the room, and she calls it a cat. The cat jumps up on the bed, and she still calls it a cat. But take the letter *b*. Turn it backward, and it is no longer a *b*. Now it is *d* and it makes a new sound and functions quite differently in words from *b*. Now turn it upside-down, and we call it *p*. Reverse it and call it *q*. In her first 5 years, the child has learned words to communicate and to name objects in a real world where directionality rarely changes the identity of an object, but this is not so in learning to read! For the first time in her life, reversing direction changes the name, the sound, and the function of these objects that we call letters of the alphabet. Combine this fact with the order of the alphabet: a, b, c, d—uh-oh. As teachers, we might introduce *d* unthinkingly before students have mastered *b* thoroughly. In other words, we can set students up for reversal problems unless we teach carefully.

The same can be said for the two most confusable vowels sounds—*e* and *i*. Stand in front of a mirror and say the short vowel sounds for *e* and *i*. Watch the mouth and feel the position of the tongue. These sounds differ, but the difference is subtle, as are the differences in the location of tongue and lips. Researchers have not presented hard and fast rules for how many instructional days to put between the letters students commonly confuse; however, several weeks of separation between the most confusable pairs makes sense and reduces students' confusion and reversals.

Teach the Short Vowel Sounds First

Vowel letters often have more than one possible sound, depending on the surrounding letters. Due to this variability, teachers and researchers agree that students have more difficulty learning the sounds for vowels than for consonants. Students who struggle with reading—particularly students with disabilities and students who have had less experience with printed words—may be confused by the multiple sounds that are possible for the vowel letters, and so they make better progress when they learn and apply just one vowel sound at a time. The rationale for teaching short vowels before long vowels is twofold: to reduce confusability and to demonstrate the rule-based nature of long vowels.

Try this demonstration: On paper, print the word *ran*. Now turn *ran* into *rain*. How did you get the short sound for the letter *a* to change to a long vowel sound? When we use a vowel combination (*ai*) to represent a long vowel sound, we introduce a new letter–sound pair, rather than an alternative sound for the letter *a*. Let's do it again. Write the word *sit*. Now change it into *sight* (or *site*). How did the sound of the *i* in the new word change? Depending on which spelling was used, the long *i* sound was determined by one of two letter combinations. In other words, *i* did not change its sound by itself; you added extra letters to make the change from a short to a long vowel sound.

Try one more: Print *cut*, and then change it to *cute*. Notice that the sound for *u* did not change all by itself. A new rule was used—silent-*e*—to change the sound for the letter *u*. If teachers begin teaching letter sounds in kindergarten, the short vowel sounds will be the most useful. That will leave plenty of reading instruction for the first-grade teacher to tackle, including the vowel and consonant clusters, the rule for an *e* at the end of short words, and the common word affixes. By the time these new possibilities are demonstrated, students will be expanding on a base of short vowel sounds that they have already learned thoroughly.

Start Teaching Letter Sounds as Soon as Possible

Years ago, teachers began reading instruction in first grade; now it is common to teach foundation skills such as phonemic awareness and letter sounds in kindergarten. Teachers have questioned whether such early instruction is developmentally appropriate.

Several comparisons of the effects of beginning phonics instruction were conducted as part of the National Reading Panel Reports of the Subgroups (2000). Comparisons between teaching phonics early (in kindergarten or in first grade) or later (in second grade and beyond) showed benefits for teaching phonics earlier, but it is important to recognize that phonics instruction for older poor readers also improved their ability to read words. Comparisons of the effects of phonics instruction in kindergarten or first grade showed similar effects across grades, which led the panel to conclude that teachers should begin teaching phonemic awareness and phonics in kindergarten to give struggling readers more time to learn. Moreover, the effects of beginning instruction in kindergarten appear to be especially strong for students who are most at risk for reading difficulties (Gersten, Darch, & Gleason, 1988). Early phonics instruction also exerts a positive effect on reading comprehension (National Report Panel, 2000), although this influence is not as strong as the effect on reading words and on spelling.

ACTIVITIES TO TEACH LETTERS AND THEIR SOUNDS

Students with reading difficulties face many hurdles early and late in the process of learning to read words. As they learn letters and sounds, discrimination among similar shapes and sounds can be a formidable task, although teachers can help by separating the confusable letters. Moreover, poor readers often need many more practice opportunities to learn new letters and sounds than do students without learning problems. Cumulative introduction of letter sounds provides the kind of practice that many students with reading difficulties need to retain the sounds they have already learned while gradually learning new letters and sounds (Gleason, Carnine, & Vala, 1991).

Begin by assessing students' current knowledge, using a checklist such as the one in Figure 4.1. Notice that the letters are not in alphabetical order. Mixing up the letter order is important because sometimes children will recite the alphabet when letters are shown to them (even when they are not in sequence), which can imply that they know the letters when they do not. Count as "learned" only the letters and sounds the student provides correctly and quickly every time he or she is asked. A set of reproducible checklists for classroom use can be found in Appendix B.

Cumulative Introduction of Letters and Sounds

After determining which letters students already know, create a small card set of the letters each student knows thoroughly. For each instructional session, choose six to eight known letters. For beginners who know no letters at all, begin with two letters that neither look nor sound the same.

Teach one new letter ("This letter is *i*, and it makes the sound /i/. The word *it* starts with *i*. Say *it* slowly." [Children: "Iiit."] "What's the first sound?" [Children: "Iii."] "Show me the letter that makes /i/."), and then add it to the set of letters already learned. Practice all of the letters and sounds several times quickly by asking students (1) to say the sound for each letter, (2) to select a letter that makes a particular sound, and then (3) to name them all again. When students can provide all sounds correctly (usually three to eight practice trials), put the set of letters aside. Conduct another activity for a few minutes, such as segment-to-spell or

Name _____ Date _____

c	f	m	b	l	e	r	t	h	u
o	p	a	k	w	j	q	n	i	x
g	v	s	y	d	z	E	I	D	L
B	J	G	N	P	A	S	R	M	F
O	Z	K	V	H	T	C	U	Y	X
W	Q								

FIGURE 4.1. Checklist for letter–sound knowledge.

decoding (below), and then return to the practice set. If students make errors, reteach the new sound. Practice again until students provide all sounds correctly. If students respond correctly without hesitation to all letters, put the set aside and return to it 10 or 15 minutes later. When students can quickly provide all of the sounds correctly two or three times in succession, they are ready for a new sound to be introduced. Each day, teachers can remove a letter that students always name correctly and rotate among known letters and sounds so that most letters are practiced daily and students have several practice opportunities for the new letter–sound correspondence.

Teaching a New Letter and Sound

The teacher selects *a, d, t, n, s, f,* and *i,* which the student knows thoroughly. She decides to teach *h,* which the student does not know. She shows the student the *h.*

TEACHER	STUDENT
This letter is *h,* and it makes the sound /h/. Say the sound /h/.	/H/.
The word *hot* starts with *h.* Say *hot.*	*Hot.*
What's the first sound?	/H/.
Show me the letter that makes /h/.	(*Touches the* h.)
(*Mixes the* h *in with the* a, d, t, n, s, f, *and* i. *Touches the* h.) What is the sound for this letter?	/H/.
(*Touches the* i.) What sound for this letter?	/I/.
(*Touches the* h.) What sound for this letter?	/H/.
(*Touches the* t.) What sound for this letter?	/T/.
(*In turn, touches the* h, a, n, h, f, s, *and* h.) What sound for this letter?	(*Provides the sound for each letter.*)

[If a student makes a mistake, the teacher can provide the correct sound instantly ("This letter says /h/") and ask the student again ("What sound for this letter?"). The teacher should return to the missed letter sound a few more times during the lesson to ensure that students receive enough practice to remember the difficult sound. When children are familiar with the routine, the teacher can touch each letter without asking children to say the sound, because they will know that they are expected to say it.]

Research has not determined a single order of introducing the letters that is superior to any other. Nevertheless, one can keep a few ideas in mind for selecting which letters to teach and which to teach next. Because vowels will require the most practice and are necessary for reading and spelling words, include a new vowel about every fourth letter. *A* and *i* are good vowels to include early in the sequence because they are easier for students to distinguish between than others and because teachers can then save *e* (often confused for *i*) for later. Because *b, d, p,* and *q* are often confused, include one of these very early in the sequence so that many other letters can be introduced in between them (I prefer *d* as the fourth or fifth letter, because it occurs more frequently in short words than *b, p,* or *q.*)

Carnine and colleagues (1997) suggest beginning with *a, m, s, t, d, i, f, r, o, g,* and *l.* Cox (1992) suggests a slightly different sequence for the first 11 letters (*i, t, p, n, s, a, d, l, f, h, g*), but notice that each sequence follows similar principles of avoiding confusability and introducing *a* and *i* as the first vowel sounds. With the 11 letters in the Cox sequence, children could learn to read and spell 120 words!

This method of direct instruction and practice through cumulative introduction is effective for many kinds of discrimination and paired-associate learning, and I will return to it in the chapter on learning sight words. Practice during cumulative introduction moves quickly, which also enhances student attention and reduces off-task behavior (Carnine, 1976).

What about the Children Who Fall Behind?

It would be convenient for teachers if all students in a group learned at the same pace, but, of course, they do not. Teachers often face the dilemma about when to introduce a new letter sound to a group when one student lags behind the others. On the one hand, we need to keep new literacy skills growing; on the other hand, children who are pushed beyond their pace of learning become confused and lose ground over time. One way to teach the lagging child effectively is through a technique called "pocket children" (O'Connor, Notari-Syverson, et al., 2005).

Most teachers dress for work with two pockets or more in their clothing, and they can make special practice sets of letters to fit in each pocket. Two pockets enable two children to receive the practice they need throughout the school day to improve the pace of their learning and the stability of their memory and retrieval of important literacy tools. Imagine teaching six beginning readers the letter sounds of the alphabet. The teacher paces instruction to introduce about two new letter sounds per week, which seems to be about right for five of the children, who are making good progress in phonics and decoding words, but one child seems to forget previously taught sounds when new letters are introduced. The teacher tells a colleague that, for this child, the letter sounds "seem to go in one ear and out the other."

Should the teacher slow the pace of instruction so that the lagging child can keep up? If so, the five other children are likely to become bored. But if the teacher continues the current pace, the sixth child may become lost among the collection of letters and sounds and perhaps even give up trying to learn to read entirely.

If many potential reading groups were available, the teacher might be able to regroup and place the child in a slightly lower, slower-paced group. But this child is already in the teacher's lowest reader group. With pocket children, the teacher can continue to include this child in the reading group but offer the child 7–10 extra practice turns each morning—the amount of practice that might enable this child to keep up with others in the group.

The teacher begins by testing the child on the letters and sounds that have been taught to see which sounds have been learned thoroughly and which are tenuous or unknown. The checklist earlier in this chapter can be used for this purpose. The teacher selects four known sounds and one from the child's tenuous or unknown collection, makes small letter cards for these letters that will fit easily into a pocket, and uses the cumulative letter-introduction strategy with this child alone in very brief instructional sessions that take about 1 minute each. The difference between cumulative letter introduction used with a reading group and the same strategy used with just one child is that teachers and children focus on the sound only for each of the letters (rather than naming the letter and its sound). The reason for focusing just on the sound is that children decode printed words by using the sounds for the letters, rather than their names.

The teacher shows the child the letter for the sound to be learned and provides the sound. "This letter says /uuu/. Say it with me." (Child and teacher: "/Uuu/.") "Now you say it." (Child: "/Uuu/.") The teacher mixes the letter *u* with four other letters the child knows thoroughly, but pulls the letter *u* to the front of the stack several times so the child gets four or more trials on *u* with one or two trials on each other letter. "Tell me all the sounds." The child provides each sound. If any are missed, the teacher provides the instructional routine again (e.g., "This letter says /uuu/. Say it with me." [Child and teacher: "/Uuu/."] "Now you say it." [Child: "/Uuu/."]), along with practice opportunities for the child to say each sound independently. This instruction takes about 25 seconds if the child names all of the sounds correctly and about a minute if the child makes errors.

When the child provides correct responses to the letter sounds several times in a row and also on a "cold session" the next day (without the teacher providing any modeled sounds), the child is ready to have a new letter sound added to the pocket set, and one of the old sounds removed. To keep these sessions brief and manageable, the card sets should contain no more than six letters—five learned sounds and one new one.

Most teachers lack the luxury of 30 minutes of time to work one-on-one with a struggling reader in the classroom, but how many times in a day do they have 25–45 seconds? How about when children enter the classroom in the morning? As children are putting away one activity and transitioning to another? When children line up for drinks or bathroom breaks? When children are working independently? Because the teacher keeps the child's letter cards in a pocket, the child does not need to be at a particular place in the classroom or even in the classroom at all. By taking advantage of these very brief practice opportunities, teachers can give a struggling reader 25 seconds of practice several times an hour over the school day.

Do you have more than one struggling reader? Do you have more than one pocket? In our research classrooms, experienced teachers easily manage two pocket children, and we have seen exceptional teachers manage up to four.

TEACHING CHILDREN TO BLEND LETTER SOUNDS TO DECODE WORDS

Although learning letter sounds is essential for decoding words, children who struggle with reading acquisition also need explicit instruction in blending letter sounds together to produce a word that they can recognize (another example of the key role that oral language plays in reading). If children have received extensive phonological awareness instruction in kindergarten, they may already know how to blend auditory sounds, which will make blending letter sounds much easier.

Among the features of decoding instruction investigated with struggling readers, how to move from letter sounds to decoding words has received considerable attention. Most reading specialists agree that children need to learn to blend letter sounds and that blending is especially difficult for students with a reading disability. Fayne and Bryant (1981) investigated the relative effects of teaching children to blend particular units of letters in words. Working with students with learning disabilities who were 7–13 years old, they taught children to blend: (1) initial bigrams with a final consonant (*co - t*); (2) onset-rime (*c - ot*); or (3) three letter sounds (*c - o - t*). Students learned the words that were taught equally well across the three conditions, but significant differences were found on the transfer lists of words that had not been taught. Children who learned to blend the initial bigrams (*fi - x*) read significantly more of the transfer words correctly than any other group.

Extending this work to younger children, O'Connor and Padeliadu (2000) compared two word-recognition strategies for struggling readers—decoding instruction using Fayne and Bryant's (1981) technique and whole-word instruction using cumulative introduction. The researchers selected the poorest readers in first-grade classrooms, half of whom were receiving special education. The researchers included equivalent amounts of letter–sound and spelling instruction in both treatments. Following 10 instructional sessions, children were tested on words that were taught during instruction and also on transfer words that had not been used in either treatment. On the immediate posttest, the groups differed on blending, which was only taught in the decoding treatment. Both groups made significant pre- to-posttest gains on letter sounds, reading the words learned in the treatments, and spelling; however, on a delayed test 2 weeks later, children who had had the decoding treatment retained more of the taught words and read significantly more of the transfer words correctly.

Two issues seem particularly relevant here. First, although many of these nonreaders were able to segment one or more sounds in spoken words, most were unable to blend isolated speech sounds prior to direct instruction in blending. Second, while children may seem to learn to read words for a short time under many different instructional conditions, the purpose of learning to decode is to be able to transfer what has been learned to new words. Only children who learned a strategy for blending letter sounds were still able to read the words weeks later.

Both of these studies used a gradual blending approach whereby children first blended a consonant and vowel and then added a final consonant. Because blending relies on auditory memory, which may also be poor for some students with disabilities (Swanson & Alexander, 2000), strategies that reduce the short-term memory load may be especially important. With this strategy, most students learned how to blend the letter sounds in one-syllable words within just a few instructional sessions.

The advantage of letter-by-letter decoding over other strategies in the early stages of reading has been firmly established (Booth & Perfetti, 2002; Ehri & Robbins, 1992; Juel & Minden-Cupp, 2000). Decoding by letter sounds has been compared to look-say methods, to instruction in word families, and to reading by analogy. All of these strategies can be useful and should be among the arsenal of strategies that children can call upon when a word is unfamiliar; however, in the early stages, letter-by-letter decoding not only helps children learn the words they are taught, but also enables transfer of decoding skill to words that have not been taught (O'Connor & Padeliadu, 2000; Share, 1995).

Relatively little comparative research among phonics approaches and programs has been conducted, and the findings suggest that the differences may be less important than the following qualities of instruction that run through all of the effective phonics approaches: Instruction should be systematic, thorough, and include extensive opportunity to apply learned skills to new words and to words in running text, such as in stories and books that use words with the taught letters and sounds (National Report Panel, 2000).

The Problem with Word Families

Good readers often enjoy examining words that have similar spelling patterns in a word family such as *might, flight, right, tight*. The problem for poor readers who practice word families as the dominant approach to reading is that they may fail to notice the sequence of letters in the list of words. Instead, they overgeneralize auditory rhyming as an effective strategy for reading (Nation, Allen, & Hulme, 2001; Treiman & Zukowski, 1988). Of course, in reading books and stories, students rarely have a handy model with which to rhyme a word. When they practiced lists in word families, they did not need to attend to the visual letter string that formed the rhyme; they only needed to look at the first letter in the word and guess the word's identity. To the teacher, the word-family approach appeared to be working within the lesson because the children said the list correctly, when all they were doing really was generating rhymes.

Unfortunately, when students see the same words in context, they will be unable to read them because they have not learned the letter string that formed the rhyme. Children who use auditory rhyming to read only look carefully at the first letter and guess a pronunciation based on the sound of the word that came before it in the list. The first-sound-and-guess approach to reading is common among older poor readers, and it is a difficult habit to break (McCandliss et al., 2003). As another example, when reading passages, older children with word-reading difficulties often overrely on language comprehension to retrieve words that they are unable or unwilling to decode in running text (Nation & Snowling, 1998). Rather than learning to decode words in the early grades, these children fail to attend to all letters in a word and instead guess a word, often based on the first letter, that could make sense in a sentence (McCandliss et al., 2003).

Phonics approaches in which students are taught all of the letter sounds systematically (and later the digraphs, diphthongs, and vowel teams such as *ch*, *oi*, and *ai*) and provided with practice blending sounds together to pronounce printed words are more effective for struggling readers than other word-reading approaches (National Report Panel, 2000). Therefore, it is recommended that teachers teach letter-by-letter decoding—also called synthetic phonics—as students' first reading strategy, followed by other strategies to augment this approach as children gain skills and confidence. Although most reading guides recommend that teachers encourage children to blend letter sounds to decode words, fewer programs show how teachers can accomplish this goal most effectively or how teachers can avoid the most common problems children experience as they learn to blend letter sounds. Blending can be an area of great difficulty for many youngsters with reading difficulties, especially if they lack a firm foundation in phonological awareness.

ACTIVITIES TO TEACH STUDENTS TO BLEND THE LETTER SOUNDS IN WORDS

Some methods of blending are more effective than others. Poor readers have two specific problems that any good approach will need to take into account. First, poor readers may have difficulty holding all of a word's letter sounds in memory long enough to sequence them correctly in pronouncing a word. Second, some words begin with consonants that have sounds that are difficult to say without a schwa (e.g., /b/ and /k/ are too often pronounced buh and kuh). If children are allowed to say these sounds with the schwa, it will be difficult to blend the consonant with the vowel that follows it (e.g., /buh/ /i/ /t/ = ???). In this section, three methods for blending that have been validated for students with reading difficulties will be demonstrated: stretching sounds together without pausing between sounds, blending the initial consonant with the vowel that follows it, and examining minimal pairs. It is important to recognize that these strategies are meant for beginning readers or older poor readers who are learning to read one-syllable words. Later chapters deal with the more complicated strategies necessary for reading multisyllabic words.

Stretching Sounds Together without Pausing between Sounds

The first method is to teach a blending strategy that does not allow a child to stop between each letter sound (Engelmann & Bruner, 1995; Gersten et al., 1988; Kuder, 1997; Lovett et al., 1994). To teach this strategy, begin with a small set of words of two or three letters that begin with vowel letters (*up, it, am*) or with consonants that generate sounds that can be stretched (*Sam, mix, lot*).

Show children the first word (*up*). Touch under the letter *u* for about two seconds, model how to say and hold the sound ("/Uuu/"), then move your finger to the letter *p* and make its sound ("/P/"). Invite children to say the sounds along with you. Repeat touching under the *u* for two seconds while making its sound, then touch under the *p* and make its sound. Guide children to say the sounds without stopping between them one or two more times and then ask them to say the word. This method is demonstrated below.

The teacher selects five or six words, in which letters that students have already learned make the sounds the students have been taught. The students have learned *a, d, t, n, s, f, i, o,* and *h*. The word list includes *sad, fin, and, not,* and *fast*.

TEACHER	STUDENTS
(*Prints* sad *on the board.*) We're going to sound this word out.	
(*Touches under the* s.) What sound for this letter?	/S/.
Good! Stretch it out.	/Sss/.
(*Moves his finger and pauses under the* a.)	/Aaa/.
(*Moves his finger under the* d *in a slow guiding motion as students say the sounds without pausing between the letter sounds.*)	Sssaaad.
Perfect! Do it again. (*Moves his finger under each letter in a slow guiding motion as students say the sounds without pausing between the letter sounds.*)	Sssaaad.
Let's say it together: Sssaaad.	Sssaaad.
What word is that?	Sad.

[If students stop between sounds or provide an incorrect sound for a letter, the teacher stops the instruction and models what the students should do. For example: "This letter (*touches under the* a) says /aaa/. Watch me sound out the word: sssaaad (*touches under each letter as he says the word*). Do it with me. Sssaaad."]

[Follow the same procedure with the remaining words: *fin, and, not,* and *fast*. Please note that to use this technique for blending, words must begin with a stretchable first sound.]

The Reading Mastery program (Engelmann & Bruner, 1995) in Appendix A is an example of a reading curriculum that uses this method to teach blending of letter sounds. In the professional development component of Reading Mastery, teachers learn to redirect children immediately if they stop between sounds and to model stretched blending. Teachers invite children to stretch the sounds in unison with them until they learn the technique. In studies that support the positive effects of this program for beginning readers (Gersten et al., 1988; Kuder, 1997), researchers suggest that stretching the sounds without stopping reduces the short-term memory and sequencing problems that plague some children with learning disabilities. Notice that this strategy is very much like the stretched blending of phonemes in Chapter 2, but here children focus on the printed string of letters as they blend the phonemes. It also shares many features with the Orton Gillingham approach (Cox, 1991; Gillingham & Stillman, 1979).

Blending the Consonant with the Vowel

Researchers and teachers agree that vowel sounds are more difficult than consonants to isolate in a spoken word. But vowels also have a useful property for blending sounds in words—all vowel sounds can be stretched. Teachers can use this feature of vowels to teach students to blend consonant–vowel combinations in which the consonant cannot be stretched. When teachers show children how to identify the vowel sound and then blend that sound with a word's initial consonant, the stretched vowel can be held long enough to blend the final sound and finish the word. This procedure for blending sounds in words that begin with unstretchable consonants is shown below.

The students have learned *a, d, t, n, s, f, i, o,* and *h.* The word list includes *hit, tan, dot,* and *hand.*

TEACHER	STUDENTS
(*Writes* hit *in large letters on the board and touches under the* i *with her right index finger.*) What sound does this letter make?	/Iii/.
(*Touches under the* h *with her left index finger.*) And this letter?	/H/.
We're going to put these sounds together. First this letter. (*Touches under the* i *with her right index finger and keeps her finger under it so that students keep making the /iii/ sound.*)	/Iii/.
Now this letter. (*Briefly touches under the* h *with her left index finger and sweeps up against the right index finger, so that the two fingers pause under the* i.)	/Hiii/.
(*As students are saying the /iii/, sweeps both fingers quickly under the* t *and off the board.*)	/T/.

Let's do it again. First this (*touches under the* i *with the right finger*).	/Iii/.
(*Touches under the* h *briefly with her left index finger and quickly sweeps to the letter* i. *As students stretch the* i, *finishes the sweep to add the sound for* t.)	Hiiit.
Say it again. (*Guides decoding with a quick touch under the* h, *a longer pause as students stretch the* i, *and a quick touch on the* t.)	Hiiit.
What word did you read?	*Hit.*

[If students have difficulty, space letters in the word a little farther apart on the board, and use the fingers of each hand deliberately as a model for how to join the letter sounds together. Some students find it easier the first few times if letter tiles are used, which can be physically moved closer together when students join the first two sounds.]

Fayne and Bryant (1981) tested multiple configurations for blending letter sounds, and found this method of blending initial consonants with vowel sounds prior to adding the last consonant to be the most effective method when it came to transferring learning to untaught words. O'Connor and Padeliadu (2000) replicated that finding. Although children can learn to read the words they see frequently through many methods—including recognizing them as unanalyzed whole words—blending is one of the few strategies that children can transfer to words they have never seen before, and, therefore, is one of the few strategies children can use to read words independently that they have not been taught to read.

Examining Minimal Pairs

When words differ by only one speech sound or phoneme (for example, *sit* and *sat*, *tan* and *ran*, or *rod* and *rot*), they are called minimal pairs (Moats, 2000). Minimal pairs can be used to help students understand that changing just one sound (represented by a letter) changes the meaning of the word, as well as its pronunciation. McCandliss and colleagues (2003) found that instruction that focused on blending letter sounds to pronounce words and then changing just one letter and blending again helped students learn to decode words and attend to all of the letters of the word in sequence. After several sessions of this kind of blending instruction, students became much less likely to guess the pronunciation of words and more likely to rely upon letter-by-letter decoding. Older poor readers (mainly second and third graders) learned to decode rapidly with this approach, which is also called Word Building (Beck & Hamilton, 2000). They transferred their learning to untaught words and also improved their silent reading comprehension over wait-listed controls (McCandliss et al., 2003). This procedure is shown below.The teacher selects letter tiles for *a, e, o, p, s,* and *t,* which are letters with sounds the students already know very well. He gives each student a set of these tiles.

TEACHER	STUDENTS
I'll show you how to make a word. Put the letter *p* in the beginning.	(*Place* p *on their work surface.*)
Put *e* in the middle. Put *t* at the end.	(*Construct the word* pet.)
What word did you make?	*Pet.*
Change the *e* to *o.*	(*Remove the* e *and replace it with* o.)
What word did you make?	*Pot.*
Change the *o* to *a.*	(*Change the letters.*)
What word now?	*Pat.*

(*Has children change one letter each time to form* sat, set, pet, pest, *and* past.)

[If students misread a word, show the word they pronounced above or below the word they should have pronounced:

    pot
    pat

By showing the words in close proximity, the teacher can direct the decoding of each word so that students see how they differ.]

In research on reading programs that have included a combination of phonemic awareness, phonics instruction, blending letter sounds to decode words, and reading the words in short stories and books, 5–10 minutes of decoding for each 30 minutes of reading instruction has generated strong reading gains for young children (e.g., Cox, 1991; Vadasy, Jenkins, Antil, Wayne, & O'Connor, 1997; Vadasy, Wayne, O'Connor, Jenkins, Poll, et al., 2005) and for older students (Lovett, Lacerenza, & Borden, 2000; McCandliss et al., 2003; O'Connor et al., 2002).

IS A WORD DECODABLE?

Teachers sometimes think of words as decodable based on the properties of the word itself, but decodability also depends on what students have been taught. In the beginning stages of decoding, simple words like *kit* or *pin* are not decodable unless students have learned that *i* usually makes the /i/ sound in short words. This issue is important because word structure is just one piece of decodability, which rests in the skills of the decoder. A word like *fish* is decodable if children have learned that *s* and *h* go together to make the /sh/ sound, but not if they have learned only one sound for each letter in the alphabet. The same could be said for a word like *right*, which is decodable only after students have learned the *-igh* pattern.

The issue of which words are decodable becomes important as teachers select books and stories for their students to read. Teachers need to think about the words in books and stories in the context of what students have learned so far, rather than to use designated grade level or terms like easy reader or decodable books to select reading materials for students in this beginning stage of reading. When teachers take into account the letter–sound combinations and the core of sight words students have learned, they can make good choices for reading materials for their students.

CHAPTER 5

Word Patterns

In an ideal world, all children would learn the alphabet letters, the most common sound each letter makes, and how to segment and blend speech sounds in kindergarten. But few teachers live in an ideal world, which is why most teachers will spend the first few weeks of first grade figuring out which children will need catch-up work in these areas and which are ready for decoding and moving into more complex word patterns. Children who need to catch up might be the first- or second-grade teacher's pocket children (see Chapter 4). Children who have learned the skills outlined in Chapters 1–4 already know how to represent more than 20 phonemes with letters (some letters overlap to represent the same phoneme(s), such as *c* and *k* as they are used most commonly). These children will be ready for the challenge of learning the letter combinations used to form the rest of the 40-odd phonemes of the English language.

We ended the last chapter with a discussion of decodability, and decodability is a good place to start the discussion of letter patterns, because the same arguments hold. For example, few teachers would suggest that -*ing* is an irregular pattern. After all, when we put -ing at the end of a word, it makes the highly regular sound we hear in *sing, thing, sewing, making,* and the like. But what about *ch*? We quickly jump to the sound heard in *chicken, chop,* and *such.* Then we begin to worry. What about the *ch* in *school*? In *Charlotte*? If *ch* makes different sounds in relatively common words, shouldn't we point out the discrepant sounds to children right from the start? If we do, then we risk losing the children who have the most difficulty learning to read, but if we don't point out the discrepant sounds from the beginning, do we risk being dishonest or, at the least, seeming to oversimplify the difficult task of reading words?

Despite the common laments that English is difficult to read and impossible to spell, empirical studies consistently find patterns of regularity in English that span the alphabetic (e.g., *m* = /m/), syllabic (e.g., *tion* = /shun/), and morphemic levels (e.g., we write *definite*, not *defanite*, because the root word is *define*). Certain combinations of letters are permissible (in Ehri's [2005] terms, "legal spellings"), and others are not. The combination *ck*, for example, can represent /k/ at the end of a word (e.g., *duck*) or in the middle of a word (e.g., *sucker*) but never appears at the beginning of a word. To demonstrate the transparency of this law of *ck*, Treiman (1998) argues that children are likely to misspell *soccer* as *socker* but rarely misspell *can* as *ckan*. Early on, exposure to printed English teaches children that even though words can be spelled in multiple ways, some ways simply are not allowable. When children learn the most common alternative letter combinations to produce a phoneme or syllable and have extensive opportunities to observe and practice these alternatives in reading and spelling words, they become increasingly sensitive to how particular patterns can be used, which is a great advantage in reading and in spelling.

One way out of the dilemma of multiple sounds for letter combinations is to teach first the most common sound that a digraph (e.g., *sh*, *ch*), vowel team (e.g., *ai* or *ee*), or diphthong (e.g., *ou* or *oi*) makes in words. If students suggest alternative sounds they have noticed in words, teachers can accept these correct alternatives ("Yes, in the word *school*, *ch* makes /k/ . . . ") and still focus on the sound of the day (" . . . but in most words, *ch* makes /ch/ as in *chicken*"). Much later, when children have learned to recognize *ch* as a unit and to read many words with the common sound for *ch*, they can explore alternative pronunciations in words that have relatively high frequencies, such as *school* or *machine*. Of course, letter combinations often change their sound due to the word's country of origin, but discussions on the origins of words are likely to be more interesting in the later elementary grades, when students have more understanding of geography and history.

As children learn the letter patterns that can represent particular phonemes, their growing knowledge of reading and spelling are mutually supportive (Ehri, 2005). Nevertheless, using letter patterns to read words is easier than using them to spell. As an example, the word *rain* cannot be read any other way because the vowel team *ai* is highly regular, but other spellings of *rain* would be legal in the English writing system, such as *rane*. Thus, even though English seems to be less decodable a language than Spanish or German, once the most common forms of letter patterns are learned, the choices for alternative pronunciations for printed words are quite limited.

One of the goals of the first 2 years of reading instruction is to establish this core of relationships between sounds and letter patterns. The overwhelming weight of the research on teaching phonics comes down in favor of teaching these graphophoneme relationships explicitly to struggling readers and suggests that explicit teaching of these relationships also helps typical learners to be better readers (National Report Panel, 2000). Once children learn all of the highly regular associations between sounds and symbols—which is the goal of phonics instruction—they use them not only to decode unknown words that are regularly spelled, but also to generate informed possible pronunciations of words with irregular spellings.

Learning to use the most common letter patterns to sound out simple words provides the scaffolding students need to recognize and retain these patterns in the more complex words they will read in the future. Ehri and Saltmarsh (1995) suggest that without learning these associations, students may get stuck in the partial alphabetic stage of reading, in which they rarely attend to medial vowels or patterns in words, making accurate spelling unlikely. To teach letter patterns, we need to help children make two conceptual shifts in their thinking about how letters capture speech sounds. They need to understand that:

- Some letter pairs make a new sound that differs from the sound made by either letter by itself. Consonant digraphs (*ch, sh, th*) and diphthongs (*ou, oy*) follow this logic, as do the letters *c* and *g* when followed by *e, i,* or *y*.
- Some letters are not connected directly to speech sounds. Rather, some letters signal changes in pronunciation of other letters in the sequence, such as the *i* to signal long *a* in *ai,* or a silent *-e* at the end of a word to change the sound of the vowel.

Teachers need to understand that as new letter patterns are introduced, children may need to be reminded that they use the new pattern the same way they would have used a single letter to decode a word. That is, letter-by-letter decoding may now be letter-pair-by-letter-pair decoding. As mentioned in the last chapter, if teachers jump too quickly to a word families approach to teach students to read words with letter patterns, struggling learners may resort to rhyming down the list of words, rather than attending to the new pattern that the teacher hopes to teach. Levy, Bourassa, and Horn (1999) taught poor readers to read words using three levels of phoneme–grapheme units: individual letters and letter-pairs, onset-rime units (word families), and whole-word units, all in conjunction with the printed words so that the patterns between spoken and printed units could be formed. Students received 4 weeks of daily word-reading instruction, in which they were required to learn a challenging 48-word training set using one of these units. When it came to generalization of the learned sounds and patterns to untaught words, performance was best in the group that learned to use individual letters and letter pairs matched to phonemes for decoding. The students in this experiment were second graders, which suggests that the benefit of teaching children to decode each letter or letter pair in a word is not limited to kindergarten and first grade.

One additional finding from Levy and colleagues (1999) has implications for reading instruction for children with reading disabilities: In a test of maintenance, they found the worst deterioration on the taught words in the onset-rime condition. This approach, also called the word families approach, is often found in basal readers in the primary grades. Although learning to read through word families (e.g., *cake, shake, snake, wake*) may be of use with average readers, it was not helpful for these remedial students who were the worst second-grade readers across the participating schools. This finding has since been replicated in a study by Christensen and Bowey (2005), in which only students who learned to decode in letter–sound units were able to transfer their learning to spelling words correctly. Contrary to expectations, children taught to decode by identifying sounds for individual letters and letter pairs also read words more quickly than those who learned to use word families.

WHICH PATTERNS TO TEACH?

At first glance, the list of potential letter patterns to teach children, along with the sounds they can make in words, may seem vast. For example, which sound should we teach for the letter pattern *-ough*? The sound we hear in *rough*? *Thought*? *Through*? Which is most common? To get us started, researchers have identified lists of the most common words in print (Hanna, Hanna, Hodges, & Rudorf, 1966; Venezky, 1999). We can use their research to identify the most frequently occurring letter patterns in high-frequency words and from those patterns identify the sounds that are used most frequently for each pattern. Over time, we can help children to understand how position in a word and the word's meaning influence its spelling (see Chapter 7). Although good readers may appreciate an exploratory approach to deducing the sounds of letter patterns (Hughes & Searle, 1997; Templeton, 1991), struggling readers who are just learning to decode words will need the same explicitness to teach letter patterns that we used to teach the letter–sound pairings for each alphabet letter (Carnine et al., 1997; Foorman, 1995).

WHICH ORDER TO TEACH THEM IN?

As with letters, there are no hard and fast rules for the order of introduction of letter patterns. Still, it makes sense to consider the complexity of the patterns and their utility for reading words. Digraphs, which are the two-letter patterns that make a unique sound (*th, ch, wh, sh*), can be introduced early because they follow the same kind of logic as single letter–sound pairings. Indeed, many of the most common words in English contain digraphs. Some vowel teams are also highly regular and several occur in the list of most common words, such as the *ee* and *ea* in *three, each*, and *years*. The diphthong *ou* also has a strong showing in lists of high-frequency words, including words such as *out, our, about*, and *around*. Therefore, rather than teach these letter combinations by class (digraph, vowel team, and diphthong), ease of instruction and immediate utility should be considered as guides. Table 5.1 shows words organized by vowel pattern, which—once the vowel pattern has been learned—will be otherwise decodable using the most common sound for each other letter that children already know.

TABLE 5.1. Letter Patterns in the 100 Most Common Words

th	or	wh	ch	ee	al	ou	er	ar
that	for	what	much	see	all	out	her	are
then	or	when	which	three	call	around	after	part
this	more	which			also			

As can be seen in the table above, the digraph *th* appears in three of the 100 most common words. Although the word *the* is the most common word in English, the *e* is spelled irregularly. Compare this frequency of occurrence with the alphabet letters *q*, *x*, and *z*, which appear nowhere among the 100 or even the 200 most common words (the word *next* ranks past word 250 in occurrence). The checklist below can be used to screen children on the most frequently occurring letter patterns (see Appendix B for a reproducible form). Note that the teacher writes in the date that the letter pattern was read correctly during the screen. Teachers can begin to screen students on these patterns after students have learned most of the common sounds for individual letters. By finding out which sounds students already know, teachers can select an appropriate pattern to include in instructional activities, such as those described in this chapter. The checklist in Figure 5.1 shows the screening in one reading group over one month's time. Blank spaces indicate that the letter pattern has not yet been learned.

ACTIVITIES TO TEACH COMMON LETTER PATTERNS

For teachers who follow the principle of teaching the most useful letters and combinations first, it makes sense to introduce *th* with the sound it makes at the beginning of short words early in the instructional sequence, perhaps before all of the letters of the alphabet are known. Such an introduction might sound like this: "When you see *th* together, it makes the sound /th/." (Teacher shows students *th* and is sure to give it the soft sound heard in *that*, *then*, and *this*.) "Say it with me." Show students a mix of letters with sounds they already know, but mix two or

	th	or	wh	ch	ee	al	ou	er	ar
Sue	1/26		1/26	2/2	2/9			2/23	2/9
Marvin	2/2		2/16		2/23				
Todd	1/26		2/16		2/23			2/2	
Takesha	1/26	2/2	1/26	1/26	1/26	2/9	2/16	1/26	2/9
Angel	1/26		2/2		2/23	2/23		2/16	2/2
Sherise	2/2	2/16	2/9	2/9	2/23			2/9	

FIGURE 5.1. Checklist of letter patterns that occur in the 100 most common words.

three *th* combinations among them (e.g., *th, a, s, th, e, t, th, m*). Ask students first to say the sound for *th* as *th* is touched in the list and then have them provide all of the sounds in the list. By mixing *th* with other letters students already know, they receive practice in which they must recall the new sound amid distractors. Show students a list of words that include *th* along with known letter sounds, such as *that, then, this, than, them.* Touch under the letters to guide children in decoding each word, as in Chapter 4. Carnine and colleagues (1997) recommend that teachers underline the *th* the first time the pattern is introduced so that students become accustomed to putting the two letters together readily. Go through the list at least twice until students are comfortable with the new sound.

To provide review of previously taught sounds, show students a list of words used in previous decoding lessons and mix three of the new *th* words in among the list (e.g., *this, sad, that, up, then, and*). For the decoding practice teachers provide each day during reading instruction, include the new letter pattern recurrently along with practice decoding words with a range of taught sounds. Research has shown that teaching students these letter combinations reduces the pool of potentially irregular words by giving students a strategy for treating words with common letter patterns as regularly spelled words (Mason, 1977).

Many children can learn a new letter pattern about every other day when review and practice are consistent. Some children who struggle with reading will need more practice decoding words and more days on a new letter pattern before the next is introduced. It is important that teachers pace their instruction to match the learning rate of the students they teach because the new pattern can be confused with the last pattern unless each pattern has been learned thoroughly. Teachers can extend practice by using sentences and stories that include multiple instances of taught letters and letter patterns, but they need to be careful that the words in the sentences and stories use the exact sound that was taught. This emphasis on consistency is the reason that the very common word *the* was not included in the practice list. Although the *th* sound is consistent with what was taught, the *e* is not. Therefore, we will teach *the* as an irregularly spelled word (see Chapter 6) or as a nondecodable sight word.

Other common words with digraphs (among the 100 most frequently used words) include *when, which,* and *much,* and all are formed from one new letter combination alongside letters that are otherwise regularly pronounced. *Wh* could make a logical next target (but note that *what* includes an irregular sound for *a*). Some students, however, could find that the similarity between *th* and *wh* causes confusion. If we follow the principle of separating the letters (letter combinations) that students might confuse, teachers might select a combination that looks and sounds quite different from *th*, such as *or* (*for, or, more*) or *ee* (*see, need, keep, tree*). Either pattern might be easier and less confusing to students than a second digraph that includes the letter *h*.

Let's assume that the teacher has taught students to recognize and provide the sound for the *th* and *or* combinations. He decides to introduce *ee*. His instruction is shown below.

TEACHER	STUDENTS
(*Writes* ee *on the board and points to it.*) These letters go together and make the sound /eeeee/. Say it with me. /Eeeee/.	/Eeeee/.
(*Adds the review patterns* th *and* or *and points to the letter combinations in random order as students provide the sound for each pattern.*)	/Th/, /ee/, /or/, /ee/, /th/.
So what sound is this? (*Points to* ee.)	/Ee/.
Good! Let's read these words. (*Shows students these words on cards or on the board*: see, seem, feet, free, tree. *Directs students to decode each word by touching under the letters in each word to encourage sounding of all letters and combinations.*)	(*Sound out each word as directed by their teacher.*)
Now let's mix it up. (*Adds words to the list that include sounds from previous lessons along with the new sound for* ee: green, that, deep, for, then, feel, this, or. *Touches under each word and gives students about 2 seconds to sound the word out, then taps the words so that all students read each word.*)	

The teacher's manual of a reading text that has adopted a word families approach might suggest that teachers introduce the letter pattern *all*, but *al* is sufficient because when children blend letter sounds and patterns without stopping between the sounds, *al* and *all* will sound the same. Moreover, *al* occurs in more words (e.g., *also, already, always,* as well as *call, fall, ball,* and *small*) and so is more useful in decoding words. Table 5.2 shows an order of introduction of letter patterns that includes sample words from the list of 500 most commonly occurring words in English. Some high-frequency words with these patterns are not included on the list because they require knowledge of rules students have not yet learned (for example, silent *e*) or because the patterns in the words do not make the sound in the word that has been taught. Words in brackets in the list include other patterns that need to be taught before the word can occur in a practice list. For example, *order* is in parentheses because it should not be included in a practice list until students have also learned the *er* pattern. Letter patterns that have consistent pronunciations but are not found in the 500 most frequent words are shown toward the end of the table. As examples, *kn, wr,* and *ph* are consistent patterns, but can wait because they occur less often. A checklist that teachers can use to monitor students' learning of these patterns can be found in Appendix B.

Of course, there are more words with these letter patterns that can be used, but the ones in Table 5.2 have special utility because of their high frequency in print. Due to their high frequency, it will be easier for teachers to find reading materials

TABLE 5.2. An Order for Introducing Letter Patterns That Takes Advantage of the 500 Most Common Words in English

th	that, this, then, than, them
or	for, form, port, [short]
ee	see, need, keep, tree, seem, week, green, free, street, deep, feet, three, feel, [wheel]
wh	which, when, wheel
ch	much, such, which, [reach], check
al	call, small, fall, always, [also]
ou	out, [about], sound, our, round, house, found, south, [hour], ground, noun, pound, thousand
er	her, letter, number, river, ever, order, better, verb, pattern, serve
ay	day, may, away, say, play, always, lay, stay
ea	each, reach, near, year, mean, read, real, sea, east, eat, hear, leave, lead, teach, clear, heat
ow	know, grow, low, slow, snow, own, [show]
ar	part, car, hard, far, start, dark, farm, mark, star
oo	look, book, good, took, wood, stood, foot
sh	fish, ship, wish, show
ol	old, told, hold, cold, gold
ing	sing, thing, king, bring, morning
oy	boy, toy
ir	girl, bird
ow	how, down, now, power, town
igh	right, high, light, might, night
ai	main, rain, wait, plain, tail, paint
oo	too, soon, food, room, moon
aw	saw, draw
oa	road, boat, soap
ur	turn, burn, hurl

Other important patterns to teach later:

au	cause, pause, haul
kn	know, knew, knee
oi	point, oil, coin, join, [voice]
qu	quick, quack, quench
ph	graph, photo
wr	wrap, wreck, wren

that incorporate these words and their patterns so that children can see and read the words in context. Two other patterns with consistent sounds are (1) the short list of very short words that end in *e*, such as *she, he, we, be,* and *me* (some teachers include *the* in this group), which form a class of their own and are among the 100 most common words; and (2) *by, my,* and *why,* which fall into the 150 most common words.

Ce, ci, cy and ge, gi, gy deserve mention because they share a rule about *c* and *g* when followed immediately by *e, i,* or *y,* but many words with these patterns contain additional features that make them difficult for beginning readers to decode (*certain, face*). Although the letter *g* uses the same rule as *c* for changing from a hard to soft sound, few examples are found among the most common words in print. Therefore, teachers can wait to teach these rules until students have already learned the most frequent and regular letter patterns.

THE SILENT-*E* RULE

About 5% of common words could be sounded out if students knew the silent-*e* (or signal-*e*, or marker-*e*) rule. After students know all of the short vowel sounds thoroughly and five or so of the letter patterns above, teachers can take 2 weeks away from patterns to teach students how to use the most common of the rules. In addition to acting as a vowel that represents a phoneme, as in *get* or *she*, the letter *e* performs several functions in English spelling, including softening the sounds of *c* and *g* (e.g., *receive, cent, garage*), and following *v* when it occurs at the end of a word (e.g., *give, love, leave, have*). Nevertheless, the most useful thing for beginning readers is to mark the change of the vowel sound from short to long, as in *mat* to *mate* or *cop* to *cope*.

Some texts introduce silent *e* through word families, such as *make, cake, shake, wake, lake*, and so forth. When that approach is used, silent *e* comes up again for *Coke, smoke, bloke* and for *bite, site, trite*; and for *cute, lute, flute*, and other vowel–consonant variations. By teaching students how the final *e* functions in words with all of the vowel letters, teachers can help students to generalize to all possible uses of the rule (Kame'enui, Stein, Carnine, & Maggs, 1981). Although it takes more time to help students acquire a generalizable rule than to teach the *-ake* family, students will also be acquiring a strategy that they can use independently when they see words that end in *e* that they have not read before.

Teaching Silent *e*

One of the clearest demonstrations of how to teach silent *e* across all its usual cases is found in Carnine, Silbert, and Kame'enui's text *Direct Instruction Reading* (1997), which draws on procedures that have received extensive research support (e.g., Kame'enui et al., 1981; Lovett et al., 1994). Rather than teach one specific pattern, the teacher first teaches the rule and then shows students a list of words, some of which end in *e* and others that do not. To teach the rule, the teacher says the rule aloud, asks the students to say it together a few times, and then to say it by themselves. Then the teacher demonstrates how to use the rule to read words. This method is shown below.

TEACHER	STUDENTS
Here's a rule: When there's an *e* at the end, the vowel says its name. Say that with me. When there's an *e* at the end, the vowel says its name.	When there's an *e* at the end, the vowel says its name.
Say the rule.	When there's an *e* at the end, the vowel says its name.
Say it again.	When there's an *e* at the end, the vowel says its name.

(Shows students a list of words.)
game
sit
hop
hope
ram
smoke

(Points to game.*)* Is there an *e* at the end?	Yes.
So will the vowel say its name?	Yes.
What's the name of the vowel? *(Points to* a.*)*	*A.*
Read the word.	*Game.*
(Points to sit.*)* Is there an *e* at the end?	No.
So will the vowel say its name?	No.
What's the sound of the vowel? *(Points to* i.*)*	/Iii/.
Read the word.	*Sit.*

(Points to the next word on the list and continues this level of guidance for all of the words on the first day of instruction. To correct errors, asks students to repeat the rule and leads students through applying the rule to the word that was read incorrectly.)

Note that not all of the words end in *e*, and so students must determine which words make use of the new rule. The teacher points to each word in turn and asks students whether the rule applies. Over the next several days, the teacher gradually reduces the amount of guidance and support, and students begin to use the rule in their head to sound out each word independently.

To use this strategy effectively, it is very important to mix words with and without a silent *e* in every lesson so that students need to think through the rule and whether it will apply in each case. We have seen what happens when teachers use lists of words that all have a silent *e* and do not ask students to determine whether the rule applies. Specifically, students tend to make every vowel long without thinking about why they are doing so. Because the words that students attempt to read later in books and stories may or may not end in *e* and may have short vowels, long vowels, or letter patterns within them, teachers who use a word-families approach risk unwittingly teaching children to stop thinking about the medial vowels in words, which have been taught so painstakingly over the last few months (McCandliss et al., 2003).

PRACTICE, PRACTICE, PRACTICE

Although some students are able to learn new letter patterns very quickly, most struggling readers will need daily practice to learn a new pattern and how to use it to read words and frequent review to retain the new patterns that were learned on previous days. Daily practice should include the letter pattern in isolation during the first few days of instruction (Show students *ou*. "Tell me the sound."), along with lists of words that have the new sound mixed among words that have other letters and patterns that students learned earlier. By mixing letter patterns in practice lists, students learn to attend to all of the letters in the word. Once a letter pattern has been learned, teachers can use the learned pattern in the mixed lists of words as new sounds and patterns are introduced so that students retain and practice all of what they have learned.

Most practice activities in the early phases of learning new letter patterns will need to be monitored closely by teachers, who can provide immediate feedback and reinforcement to keep students focused. Practice with teachers ensures that students learn the new sounds correctly and that any potential for mislearning a letter sound or letter pattern is avoided. As students demonstrate competence with a new letter pattern, some of the practice time can be shared with teaching assistants, tutors, or peers who are capable of providing assistance and feedback.

The ultimate practice for all of the sound–symbol associations is the practice students gain by reading words in running text, including sentences, stories, and books. By selecting reading materials that incorporate the taught patterns, teachers help students to review and retain taught patterns in natural and agreeable ways. By teaching students the letter patterns that occur most frequently in text, along with using high-frequency words as part of the daily practice of reading words, students will find the time spent reading much more enjoyable. Orchestrating these opportunities will be the topic of Chapter 8.

CHAPTER 6

Developing Sight Words

The term "sight words" refers to the core of words that children recognize instantly when they see them in print. How they get recognized instantly is the topic of this chapter. Two kinds of sight words will be considered: words that can be decoded but have been learned so well that students do not need to sound them out any longer and words that cannot be sounded out because their spellings are irregular and, therefore, must be learned through other means. Both kinds of words are important, and both have received considerable attention in instructional research. Let's take each type in turn.

DECODABLE SIGHT WORDS

Words that are decodable can be regarded as sight words when they are among the most frequently occurring words in printed English because reading these words quickly and easily is necessary for fluent reading to develop. Ehri (2005) makes no distinction between words that are and are not decodable in her discussion of the importance of building a large core of words that are recognized without conscious effort. Rather, she suggests that words become sight words when their spellings and pronunciations are stored firmly in memory. By the time that sight words can be recognized instantly, reading them no longer requires attention to decoding because the spelling and pronunciation have become unitized—that is, no attention is paid to the word parts. Students continue to see all of the letters (and to recognize when letters are missing), but they do not need to take time to sound out each letter.

The process by which words are stored so completely is a result of a series of connections that occur at various levels, including individual letters and their sounds, letter patterns such as those described in the last chapter, syllable parts (sometimes called chunking), and whole words. The storage of these various units becomes possible when students have sufficient letter–sound connections to make particular units useful (e.g., the *er* in *letter*).

HIGH-FREQUENCY WORDS WITH IRREGULAR SPELLINGS

Not all words can be decoded by using letter sounds and patterns because some spellings break the rules children have been taught to use. Even some very common words have spellings that defy conventions, such as *they*, *said*, *to*, and *there*. Researchers have noted that children with reading disabilities sometimes read these irregularly spelled words as accurately as words that can be decoded, partly because they lack the skills to use different methods for reading different words. It is important to realize that by "as accurately as," what researchers have found is that students with reading disabilities don't read either kind of word very well.

Teachers sometimes have difficulty recognizing irregular words because they occur so frequently in text materials for beginning readers. Moreover, some words use common spellings but unusual pronunciations. For example, it is easy to see that *said* is not spelled as it sounds but more difficult to spot the words *put*, *son*, or *was* as spelled irregularly because the consonant–vowel–consonant pattern seems so easy to read and spell. It is not surprising that we view words that occur frequently as decodable because we see them so often that we read them without any conscious thought. Estimates suggest that the 25 most common words make up nearly one third of the text that beginning readers see and that the 100 most common words make up nearly half of the words in print (Fry, Kress, & Fountoukidis, 2000). It is worth the time for teachers to slow down and attempt to sound out words that will be shown to students so that teachers know whether to treat the word as decodable.

The distinction between decodable and irregular words is important when we select the cues that we give to students. "Sound it out" will not generate a correct pronunciation for an irregularly spelled word, and "Look at the first letter. Can you guess the word?" is dangerous because guessing from the first sound is such a difficult habit to break once students begin to use it. In addition, guessing words from context is a notoriously unreliable process (Adams, 1990).

Reading words with irregular spellings is sometimes called orthographic reading to distinguish it from phonological reading methods (i.e., decoding), in which words are read by translating individual letters and letter patterns to their phonemes (Torgesen et al., 2001). The spellings of irregular words contain clues to their pronunciation, but some of the letters may generate uncommon sounds or no sounds at all, such as in the word *yacht*. The *y* and *t* make their usual sounds, *a* makes one of its frequent alternative sounds, and students must learn to recall the odd *ch*, which they can do after multiple exposures and opportunities to study the word. Teachers would need to provide these exposures and opportunities, since *yacht* is rare relative to other words in our language, and so few chances arise to learn the word through its natural occurrence in books. Because words with irregular spellings still offer clues to their identities, it is helpful to students when teachers require them to examine all letters in these words and to determine how each letter functions to contribute toward the pronunciation of the word.

RELATIONS BETWEEN DECODING AND THE DEVELOPMENT OF SIGHT WORDS

So when might students establish a basic core of words that they recognize instantly? High-frequency words like *the*, *is*, and *of* become sight words relatively quickly because they occur on nearly every page of text that students read. However, most words that we can read by sight appear less often than that. Individuals must read extensively in order to encounter specific words often enough to speed their recognition. Individuals differ greatly in their amount of independent reading (Anderson, Wilson, & Fielding, 1988), and those who avoid reading encounter and learn fewer words. That is why it is so important that teachers ensure that their students all read as many words as can be managed through daily reading instruction.

To illustrate the importance of decoding skill on the development of sight-word knowledge, Reitsma (1983) gave repeated exposures to new words to first graders at the beginning of and midway through the first-grade year. Midway through first grade, after students had acquired some decoding skill, they decreased the time it took to recognize words with as few as four repetitions, and more repetitions continued to decrease the time it took for students to identify words. At the beginning of the year, when students had received much less decoding instruction, four exposures had no effect on decreasing word-recognition time. Reitsma concluded that decoding skill was necessary for a sight-word core to develop. Compton (2000) furthered that argument by finding a high correlation (.70) between decoding skill and word identification in general, a correlation that appears to increase under timed conditions (Jenkins, Fuchs, van den Broek, Espin, & Deno, 2003)

Some of the most convincing evidence for the important role of decoding ability for developing sight-word knowledge comes from studies of words with irregular spellings. Tunmer and Chapman (1998) found that students may be skilled in irregular-word reading and in decoding, or skilled in neither. Some students can decode well but still perform poorly on words with irregular spellings, perhaps because they lack adequate exposure to these words and sufficient reading practice. The necessary relationship that ties decoding to reading irregular words is revealed by the observation that only skilled decoders are skilled irregular-word readers (Gough & Walsh, 1991). Thus, decoding skill appears to be important for learning all kinds of words, whether regularly or irregularly spelled.

These arguments explain the organization of this book, with the emphasis in Chapters 2–5 on developing the skills needed to decode words. Once students have these skills, it is likely that they will already have several sight words in their repertoire, such as the 25, 50, or 100 most frequently occurring words. Many good sources of high-frequency words are available, including *The Reading Teacher's Book of Lists* (Fry et al., 1993), *The American Heritage Word Frequency Book* (Caroll, Davies, & Richman, 1972), the research reports of Venezky (1999) and Hanna, Hanna, Wilson, and Roudorf (1966), and websites that are easy to find by conducting a search for 100, 500, or 1,000 common words. Ordering information for some of these resources can be found in Appendix A.

These lists overlap considerably. For example, the 150 most frequent words of Caroll and colleagues (1972) include all but 11 of the 100 words children most commonly use in their writing during the primary years, according to Hillerich (1978). The 11 words children use in writing that are not among the 150 most common words fall within the next 100 words on lists by Caroll and website high-frequency lists (i.e., *because, got, saw, home, house, mother, school, don't, am, didn't, us*). Table 6.1 shows 200 common words in order of frequency to get teachers started. This list comprises words that occur across several of the dominant lists drawn from the researchers listed above and can be broken into sets of 25 to 50 words to use as a screening device to determine the words students already know and to identify good places to begin instruction and practice for building a core of sight words. Reproducible screening checklists of these words in sets of 50 can be found in Appendix B. With the exception of *got, didn't*, and *don't*, these common words in reading also include the 100 words that students use most often in their writing.

ACTIVITIES TO TEACH STUDENTS TO READ SIGHT WORDS

Students who are average readers tend to pick up sight words from repeated exposure to the words in books and stories. Struggling readers and students with reading disabilities are likely to need frequent small doses of instruction so that they develop a core of words they can read effortlessly.

Effective strategies for teaching sight words are described in the remainder of this chapter. Many of the same principles recommended for teaching letters and their sounds apply when teaching high-frequency words. In particular, introduce new words cumulatively and practice the new word in isolation, in lists among known words, and in the context of books and stories. Review words daily until they are learned thoroughly (that is, until children have read the word correctly over multiple opportunities and instructional sessions). As with letters and letter combinations, avoid teaching confusable words such as *was* and *saw* during the same instructional session. Regardless of the technique used to introduce new sight words, teachers should be aware that many children will need extensive and fre-

TABLE 6.1. 205 Commonly Occurring Words in Printed English

the	which	did	think	still
of	their	down	also	name
and	said	only	around	should
a	if	way	another	home
to	do	find	came	give
in	will	use	come	air
is	each	may	work	line
you	about	other	three	mother
that	how	don't	words	set
it	up	didn't	must	world
he	out	water	because	own
for	then	long	does	under
was	she	little	part	last
on	many	very	even	read
are	some	after	place	never
as	so	word	well	am
with	these	called	such	us
his	would	just	here	left
they	then	where	take	end
at	into	most	why	along
be	has	know	things	while
this	more	get	help	sound
from	her	through	put	house
I	two	back	years	might
have	like	much	different	next
or	him	before	away	below
by	see	go	again	saw
one	time	good	off	something
had	could	new	went	thought
sat	no	write	old	both
not	make	our	number	few
but	than	used	side	those
what	first	me	great	school
all	been	man	tell	show
were	its	too	men	always
when	who	any	between	looked
we	now	day	say	large
there	people	same	small	often
can	my	right	every	together
an	made	look	found	ask
your	over	got	big	turn

quent practice before they recognize these words instantly across contexts. Keep in mind that instruction and practice on quick recognition of sight words (as with learning all kinds of words) should be just one part of a complete reading lesson that also includes instruction in decoding words, reading connected text, reading comprehension, and writing.

Constant Time Delay

Constant time delay procedures can be used to help students learn to read sight words. This procedure requires several learning trials on a small set of about five new words. During the first instructional trial, teachers show students words one at a time, provide the word, and wait 3 seconds, after which students respond by saying the word. After the first trial, teachers mix up the words, hold them up one at a time, and pause for 3 seconds for the students to identify the word. If students identify the word correctly, teachers praise briefly and show the next word. If students do not respond within 3 seconds, teachers provide the word and point out some memorable feature (e.g., "Notice the -ey at the end of they."). Teachers then have students wait 3 seconds before they say the word. Teachers repeat these practice and feedback opportunities for the word set several times until students identify all of the words correctly at least twice. On subsequent days, teachers review words to ensure that students retain them. Once learned, the words can be incorporated in practice sets and used in games such as those described later in the chapter. The procedure for constant time delay is shown below.

TEACHER	STUDENT
I'm going to read some words, one word at a time. You'll watch the words. When I point to you, you'll read it. Here's the first word. (*Holds up the card with the word* what *on it.*) Look at the word until I point to you. This is *what.* (*Waits 3 seconds and then points to the child.*)	(*Looks at the word.*) What.
(*Puts the card on the back of the stack and reads the next card.*) This is *all.* (*Waits 3 seconds and then points to the child.*)	All.
(*Puts the card on the back of the stack and reads the next card.*) This is *were.* (*Waits 3 seconds and then points to the child.*)	Were.
(*Puts the card on the back of the stack and reads the next card.*) We. (*Waits 3 seconds and then points to the child.*)	We.
(*Puts the card on the back of the stack and reads the next card.*) Your. (*Waits 3 seconds and then points to the child.*)	Your.
(*Shuffles the cards, shows the child the card* we, *waits 3 seconds and points to the child.*)	We.

Good! (*Shows the card* all, *waits 3 seconds and points to the child.*)	*All.*
Great! (*Shows the card* your, *waits 3 seconds and points.*)	I don't remember.
(*To correct an error, the teacher reads the word, points out a memorable feature, waits 3 seconds, and points to the child.*) This card says *your*. See how it starts with the word *you*?	
Your. (*Waits 3 seconds and points to the child.*)	*Your.* It starts like *you*.
That's right. Read this card when I point to you. (*Shows* were, *waits 3 seconds and points to the child.*)	*Were.*
That's right. (*Follows this procedure for* what.)	*What.*
Yes. (*Shuffles the five cards and gives the child 3 seconds to read each card. When the child has read all five cards correctly twice, the teacher praises the child and reviews a few of the cards from the previous week.*)	

Variations on the constant time delay procedure have been used in special education settings to teach students to identify words (Bradley, 1975; Wolery, 2002), to spell them (Coleman-Martin & Heller, 2004), to learn math facts (Wolery et al., 1992), and to learn behavioral responses (Wolery, 2002). If students take more than five learning trials to learn the new words, teachers can either reduce the number of words in the practice set or use games such as Concentration or Bingo, which require students to select a printed word spoken by the teacher rather than to produce the spoken word from memory or to use decoding skills.

Spelling Words Aloud

Children who have difficulty reading words often fail to attend to the word's medial patterns—the vowels and letter combinations that occur in the middle of the word (McCandliss et al., 2003). Saying the letter names aloud as students study the word can focus their attention on all of the letters in sequence, which then encourages students to notice the letters that are responsible for particular sounds in words (Carnine et al., 1997). To use this strategy, show students a short list of words (about three new words and two or three review words). While pointing at each word, say the word aloud for students to repeat, direct students to say all of the letters in the word as they examine it, and have them say the word aloud again. Repeat for each word in the list.

Next, go back to the beginning of the list and ask students to read each word without you reading it first. If students read the word correctly, continue through the list. If students misread a word, correct the error by reading the word aloud and direct students to spell it as they examine it and to say the word aloud again. Continue the spelling aloud of each word as corrective feedback until students can read the entire list of words correctly without teacher prompting.

Last, point to the words in random order for a final quick test of reading accuracy. If students have difficulty, repeat the spelling aloud stage after modeling reading the word. If students read the words correctly in random order, these words can be used as review words in future lists. This procedure is shown below.

The teacher shows students the following list of three new words and three review words:

water

long

little

other

find

some

TEACHER	STUDENT
(*Points at the first word.*) This word is *water*. Look at it and spell it. What word was that?	*W-a-t-e-r. Water.*
(*Points to* long.) This word is *long*. Look at it and spell it. What word was that?	*L-o-n-g. Long.*
(*Points to* little.) This word is *little*. Look at it and spell it. What word was that?	*L-i-t-t-l-e. Little.*
(*Follows the same procedure for* other, find, *and* some.)	(*Spell aloud as they look at each word and then read the word.*)
Now let's read the words. (*Points to* water.) Read this.	*Water.*
(*Points to* long.) Read this.	*Long.*

(*Points to the remaining words as students read them aloud.*)

[If students make an error, ask them to look at the word, tell them what it is, and ask them to spell the word aloud and then read it. Then go back to the beginning of the list and give students another opportunity to read the entire list accurately. Use spelling the word aloud to correct any additional reading errors on the list.]

Sets of Words with Unusual Spellings

Some high-frequency words share spelling patterns, such as short words that end in the letter *e* (*be, he, me, she, we*), the unusual but common words with *-ould* (*could, should, would*), the long-*i* sound spelled with *igh* (*right, high, night, light, might*), the -*other* pattern (*other, another, mother, brother*) and final *s* pronounced as *z* (*is, his, as, has, was*). These words can be clustered to demonstrate the letter pattern that forms the sound and then practiced by using the spelling aloud, word wall, or constant time delay methods. This procedure is demonstrated below and practiced with constant time delay.

The teacher arranges the following words cards in a vertical column on a table:

by

my

cry

fly

why

TEACHER	STUDENT
Let's look at these words. How do they all end?	In *y*.
Yes. In these short words, the *y* at the end says /iiiii/. Make that sound.	/Iiiii/.
Yes. I'm going to read each word, and when I point to you, you'll read it.	
(*Points to* by.) This word is *by*. (*Waits 3 seconds, then points to the students.*)	*By.*
(*Points to* my.) This word is *my*. (*Waits 3 seconds, then points to the students.*)	*My.*
(*Follows this procedure for all the cards and then picks them up and shuffles the order. The teacher shows each word card for 3 seconds and then points to a student to read it. If students make errors, the teacher reminds them of the* y *at the end.*)	
The *y* at the end says /iiiiii/. Make that sound.	/Iiiiii/.
So this word is *ffflllyyy*. Read it.	*Fly.*
(*Shuffles the cards and continues to provide reading opportunities and corrections until students read through all the cards correctly twice.*)	

Word Walls and Word Banks

Both of these methods provide ways for teachers to collect words that have been taught and learned so that students can practice them frequently. For word walls, the teacher organizes learned high-frequency words in lists either alphabetically (for example, *the, them, then, there, they*) or by letter patterns (for example, *right*, *high, night, sight, light*), and posts the words prominently on a wall of the classroom. Students can practice the lists with peers or teachers or can find words they wish to use and spell correctly in their writing (Castagnozzi, 1996).

Word banks serve a similar function, but rather than using the same list for all students in the class, teachers can select words that individual students have learned and create a unique set of word cards for each student who is learning sight words. The cards are collected in a box so that students can practice them individually or with a more capable reading peer. Because each word bank is determined by the particular words each student has learned, different rates of learning can be accommodated with practice materials that are appropriate for each learner.

Word banks or word walls can be turned into alphabetized spelling lists by typing the words into a data processing program such as Excel and using the automatic alphabetizing function of the program. Each time students have learned to read several new words, the words can be added to the list and realphabetized to make finding the word easier. In this way, students can be held accountable for words they have learned to read and spell in their own writing.

Speeded Word Recognition

The goal of learning to read high-frequency words is to recognize them quickly without extensive deliberation. Therefore, after words have been learned to a high rate of accuracy (for example, when students read the word correctly on several consecutive days without teacher assistance), students should be encouraged to read the words as quickly as they can under timed conditions. Teachers can create a new randomly ordered list each time students learn about 25 new words. Although optimal rate of reading high-frequency words has not received extensive research attention, most students should be able to recognize these words in lists within 1 second (a rate of 60 words per minute) and transfer that rate of recognition to the same words when they read them in stories and in other contexts. By recognizing common words quickly and easily, students will be able to devote their attention and energy to more difficult words and to the phrasing of words in sentences and paragraphs, which generates the meaning of the material they read.

Practice Games

Once learned, sight words will receive considerable and naturally occurring practice as children read books and stories because these words account for more than half of the words in printed materials for readers in the primary grades (Zeno, Ivens, Millard, & Duvvuri, 1995). Words can also be reinforced following instruction through games such as Concentration, Bingo, and Beat the Clock.

Concentration can be played in small groups of two to six students. This game can be used with beginners who only know 10–20 sight words or with students who have more reading ability as a means to review words from larger word sets. Teachers make two word cards for each word students are to practice. Turn the cards face down and arrange them randomly on a table. The first player turns over a card, reads the word aloud, then turns over one additional card and reads that word aloud. If the pair of words match, the child keeps both cards. If they do not match, the child puts them back on the table face down, and the next player turns over a card, reads the word on it, and has one opportunity to try to locate its match. As students learn where particular words are located in the random array, words receive multiple repetitions. The game continues until all cards have been matched, and the winner is the child who has gathered the most cards.

Bingo is played with 25 words at a time. The playing cards have 25 words arranged in a 5×5 array, and each card should have the same words in different arrays. These playing cards are easily constructed by using the table function of a word-processing program to create a five column, five row table. The teacher types the 25 words into the grid with a different order for each of the playing cards. The 25 words are also printed individually on cards to form the drawing pile. Children take turns drawing and reading one word aloud. All students search for the word on their card and cover it with a disk or bean. Children continue taking turns drawing and reading a word aloud until one child has five words in a row. To verify a winning row, the child must read all five words correctly as students ensure that the five words were among those that were drawn. Teachers can increase the difficulty of the game by constructing the 5×5 array of words as a random selection from a drawing pile of 35–50 words the students are learning. A sample set of four playing cards with the 25 most common words can be found in Appendix B.

Beat the Clock can be played in pairs or small groups and can focus on reading or writing words quickly. Both versions require a checker (either a listener or spell checker), and in both versions students attempt to beat their own records, rather than playing competitively against each other. For the reading version, the checker holds a stopwatch or countdown timer, and the player reads as many words from a word bank or a set of high-frequency word cards as possible in 1 or 2 minutes. The checker shows the word and judges correctness by placing the cards in a correctly read or incorrectly read pile. When the time is up, the correct cards are counted and recorded, and that becomes the number that the player tries to beat the next time the game is played. Words missed can be used in reteaching and practice sessions.

To play Beat the Clock as a spelling game, learned words for each student playing the game are printed onto cards and shuffled. The checker sets the countdown timer or monitors the stopwatch for 2 or 3 minutes. Each player draws one card at a time and writes the word. As soon as one word is completed the child draws another card and continues copying words rapidly until the time is up. The checker checks the spelling and legibility of each word and counts the number of correctly spelled and legible words. This number of words is compared to the last time the game was played, and each child that beats his or her own previous number of correct words wins. Children are allowed to view the word while they are spelling it, but as they learn words more thoroughly they will need fewer peeks at the word to retain it in memory, which helps them to increase their score over time.

It should be clear by now that some students will need considerable practice with high-frequency words before they are retained as sight words. The rewards for learning these words thoroughly and reliably are smoother, less effortful reading and perhaps a greater inclination to read independently (which in turn may also increase a student's store of instantly recognized words).

CHAPTER 7

Reading Multisyllabic Words

I wonder whether this has ever happened to you? I come across a new word and attempt a pronunciation in my head. I try it in the sentence I am reading, it seems to make sense, and so I keep on reading. I have a good memory, so I might automatically supply this pronunciation for the word the next time I see it in print. Over time it becomes part of my reading vocabulary. Then I hear an articulate speaker use the word but with a different pronunciation than the one I generated for my own use (of course, this is more embarrassing if I have also integrated this new word into my speech). My first impulse is to rehearse the word in my head by segmenting it into its speech sounds and trying to retrieve a spelling, so that I can match the segmented form with the letters used to represent each part. I want to know where I went wrong! My next impulse is to look the word up in the dictionary to verify the spelling, to segment the written components into pronounceable units, and to check which one of us is pronouncing the word correctly. If the speaker I heard was correct, I instantly transform that word's pronunciation in my memory, rehearse it in my mind, and then apply that new pronunciation the next time I read the word. Presto! The error has been repaired.

But what if I were unable to break the word apart and to retrieve a spelling for the word? This loop of comparison of spoken words to written forms and written to spoken words becomes very difficult, if not impossible. The problem is exacerbated when words have several syllables. I may decide to give up on these long words and cease attempting to read them.

We do not want our students to give up on long words. Therefore, we will need to teach students how to break apart long words into manageable segments

that can be used for decoding words, for spelling them, and for comparing syllables and morphemes across words with similar spellings. As words become longer,
even students who have mastered basic decoding will need new strategies for
reading words. Some of the strategies they learned for reading short words, such as
how the -*e* at the end of a word signals a long vowel, take on alterations in longer
words. For example, the silent *e* in a base word is dropped when suffixes that begin
with vowels are added (as, for example in *packaging* or *television*).

Much of what students need to learn about longer words is based on rules and
so relationships between letters and their sounds are influenced by their position in
words and by other letters around them. The variations among letter sounds based
on these dependencies give us the impression that English is spelled more irregularly than it is. Although about 10% of words in English have spellings that are
only loosely related to the word patterns that students typically learn in their first
years in school, most words that students see in print can be read by beginning
with word patterns and adding a few rules for combining word parts.

It is true that spelling words is more difficult than reading them. To understand why this is so, consider the long *o* sound. When students see words that have
the letter pattern *oa*, that pattern is nearly always pronounced as a long-*o* sound.
But if students want to spell the long *o* they hear in a word, they could choose *oa*, or
add a silent -*e*, or try the -*ough* they hear in *thorough*. In words with several syllables, word parts may have been joined from different languages of origin, which
further complicates spelling.

Reading words with several syllables has long been recognized as a stumbling
block for students with reading difficulties (Rack et al., 1992; Shefelbine, 1990;
Spear-Swerling & Sternberg, 1994). Students who usually read aloud in strong
voices may nevertheless quietly mumble over these words and hope that no one
will notice their inability to read them. Other students will stop mid-sentence with
a questioning look and hope that a teacher or peer will provide the word so that
they will not need to try to decipher it for themselves. Teachers may be willing simply to provide the word because they are not sure how to teach students to read
long words independently.

In fact, observational studies of classroom practice find few instances of teachers teaching students strategies for decoding these words (Vaughn et al., 1998), and
interviews with teachers suggest that they lack training in how to teach students to
read long words (Bos et al., 2001; McCutchen & Berninger, 1999). Good readers
seem to glean the rules for long words from multiple exposures to particular words
in the materials they read. Researchers have estimated that most of the conventions
that students learn about syllabification come from reading words repeatedly in
context. As students read, they begin to understand that a combination such as *dn*
is more likely to signal a break between two syllables than the combination *dr*,
which usually functions as a blend within a syllable (Cunningham, 1998).

For poor readers who have less exposure to printed words, instruction that
includes affixes and common syllables is essential. The frequency with which par-

ticular word parts are encountered influences the likelihood that readers will recognize or be able to decode a word correctly, and multisyllabic words often have affixes that can be separated from roots to ease the decoding burden. Nagy, Anderson, Schommer, Scott, and Stallman (1989) suggested that knowledge of how word forms combine, along with recognition of morphologically related words (they estimate 88,533 distinct word families in printed school English), could enhance both decoding and understanding the meanings of unfamiliar words that students encounter in print.

A series of studies explored the extent to which knowledge of prefixes, suffixes, and root words could transfer to word identification when instruction is strategic. Shefelbine (1990) found that poor readers rarely attend to all letters, or even all syllables, in multisyllable words. Yet just 5 hours of focused instruction on using vowels and affixes in multisyllable words, spaced over 30 days, significantly improved the decoding performance of fourth- and sixth-grade poor readers. Moreover, these students transferred the word parts they had learned to words that contained these parts, but were not part of the instruction.

Lenz and Hughes (1990) developed a model of word-recognition strategy instruction that was effective for students with reading disabilities in the middle school years. The DISSECT model (*D*iscover the context, *I*solate the word's prefix, *S*eparate the word's suffix, *S*ay the word's stem [or base word], *E*xamine the word's stem, *C*heck with another person to see if you are correct, *T*ry to find the word in the dictionary) was designed to provide a collection of flexible strategies for students who lacked a strong decoding base. The step in part 4—say the word's stem—was central to this strategy. This step introduced the rule of twos and threes to decode the base word, which often has more than one syllable aside from the attached affixes. The researchers taught students that if a stem begins with a vowel, separate the first two letters; if a stem begins with a consonant, separate the first three letters, then say the syllable. Students were to repeat the process until the whole stem had been recognized. Once the stem was recognized, the affixes were added back on so that students could pronounce the whole word. The instructional routine included teacher modeling of the entire strategy, paraphrasing of each step by students, memorizing the steps, and then several weeks of controlled practice and feedback on the individual steps and on combining all the necessary steps for reading an individual word. To learn this procedure thoroughly required 20–25 minutes at least three times per week over a 6-week period.

In our work (O'Connor et al., 2002; O'Connor & Bell, 2004; O'Connor et al., 2005), an abbreviated version of DISSECT was also successful in teaching students with reading disability in third, fourth, and fifth grade to decode multisyllabic words. Our strategy, called BEST (*B*reak apart the word, *E*xamine each part [or base word], *S*ay each part, *T*ry the whole thing in context), captured some of the steps in the DISSECT model. BEST word analysis instruction took 5–10 minutes daily as part of a 30-minute tutoring session, and students began to generalize the strategy independently in about 3 weeks.

Several sources can provide the materials for teaching the commonly occur-ring word parts used in strategies like DISSECT and BEST. White, Sowell, and Yanagihara (1989) reanalyzed Caroll and colleagues (1972) list of common words to derive the affixes that appeared in words most frequently. In their research, a col-lection of just 20 prefixes accounted for 97% of all word prefixes, and 16 suffixes for 87% of the suffixes in words. You can find these affixes in Tables 7.1 and 7.2. White, Power, and White (1989) used this information to improve the reading and spelling ability of students with disabilities. Glass Analysis (Glass, 1973) provides lists of sequentially more difficult words containing common orthographic patterns (e.g., *rain, strain, detaining, container*). These lists can help students make use of the redundancies in printed English. Redundancy of word parts across words becomes even clearer when word-analysis instruction includes information about English morphemes (Carlisle, 1987; Dixon & Engelmann, 1980), which are the meaningful parts of words and include affixes such as *re-* (meaning to do it again) and *-less* (meaning without) along with base words.

Another approach for older students with word-reading difficulties is word building. Although word building has been recommended as an instructional strategy for many years (e.g., Beck & Hamilton, 2000; Cunningham, 1998), it has recently been tested through a series of experiments conducted by McCandliss and colleagues (2003). In their first experiment, they identified the patterns of errors that were made most commonly by students with reading disabilities in the intermediate grades. These students accurately made use of the first letter in a word, followed by relatively worse decoding of the remaining vowels and con-sonants. Their strategy was to teach students to attend to the medial and final sounds by progressive minimal pairing of words that differed by only one letter. After 20 sessions of instruction and practice, students read significantly more nonsense words than those in the control group, but also generalized words in the training set to real words outside the training set, including words with more than one syllable.

ACTIVITIES TO TEACH STUDENTS TO READ MULTISYLLABIC WORDS

As described above, several effective methods have been validated in experimental studies for helping students read long words. The remainder of this chapter pres-ents tables of the word parts that will be most useful to teach and procedures for teaching several specific strategies so that students will be able to build a flexible core of strategies that will unlock most printed words in English.

Research findings consistently favor teaching affixes to students with reading difficulties. Although lists differ somewhat across studies, all agree that students will need assistance to break down long words into more manageable parts. One of the most obvious and useful approaches is to teach common affixes by using the same direct teaching strategies recommended for teaching the letter sounds, digraphs, diphthongs, and vowel teams. Inflected verb forms such as *-ing* and *-ed*, and plural noun forms ending in *-s* and *-es* are reasonable places to begin because they occur very frequently in words.

Teachers should be aware that these inflected endings may have different pronunciations, depending on the words to which they are added. As an example, *-ed* (which is among the most common word endings) can be pronounced as /t/ or as /ed/. Compare pronunciations of *-ed* in *stopped* and *ended*. Students without a good ear for correct usage may need many demonstrations before they will be able to discriminate between the various pronunciations of *-ed*. Moreover, even simple word endings with regular pronunciations like *-ing* frequently change the base word by dropping an *-e* (as in *making*) or doubling a consonant (as in *dropping*). Because of these fluctuations in spelling, rules for dropping final *-e* and doubling consonants should be incorporated along with the strategies for breaking apart long words.

COVER AND CONNECT

Instruction in breaking down longer words can begin unambiguously with the recognition of compound words (e.g., *into, doghouse, baseball*). Teaching students to find the little words in longer words is a useful first step because the same approach is encouraged in more complex strategies such as BEST and DISSECT when students become more sophisticated readers.

Although spelling words with inflected endings requires knowledge of rules, reading words with endings that include *-ing* and *-ed* verbs (ask*ing*, plant*ed*), plurals or possession (dog*s*, dress*es*, her*s*), or comparisons (old*er*, old*est*) are much easier, and words with these variations appear often in the printed materials students read in first grade and beyond. Show students first how to look for these endings and then how to detach or cover these endings. With this simple strategy, they will be able to read the base word and then connect the ending back to read the whole word.

Many first-grade words also end with the unaccented /l/ sound found in words like *little, puzzle,* and *puddle*. Because the first syllable is often decodable using the most common sounds for alphabet letters, the same strategy used for inflected endings (cover the *-le*, read the first syllable, uncover, and connect the whole word) usually elicits a correct pronunciation of these two-syllable words. The list of *-le* endings includes: *-ble* (*crumble, tremble*), *-fle* (*baffle, duffle*), *-tle* (*bottle, little*), *-dle* (*puddle, middle*), *-gle* (*jingle, juggle*), *-kle* (*twinkle, sparkle*), *-ple* (*purple, dapple*), and *-zle* (*puzzle, dazzle*). Of course, if the first syllable is open (*ma-* in *maple*; *bu-* in *bugle*) the vowel is long, and so it might be best to save these examples for instruction in the six syllable types (described later in this chapter), which can occur in second or third grade or later for older poor readers. The analysis of compound words, inflected endings, and words that end in consonant *-le* can help students to bridge to other kinds of morphemes that change the meaning of a word.

Teaching Affixes and Morphemes

The research of White, Power, et al. (1989) has provided useful guidelines for beginning to teach students to recognize prefixes and suffixes, which are also morphemes, or meaningful word parts. In their analysis of common words in print, they found that 58% of all words with prefixes were accounted for with the four prefixes *un-*, *re-*, *in-*, and *dis-*. Among the suffixes, the inflections on verbs (*-ing*, *-ed*) and nouns (*-s*, *-es*) account for more than 60% of word endings, with the next most common endings including *-ly*, *-er/or*, *-sion/tion*, *-ible/able*, *-al*, *-y*, and *-ness*. Many researchers recommend teaching the meanings of these word parts along with their pronunciations to assist with vocabulary development (Carlisle, 2004). It is likely that some of the meanings of these very common affixes will be apparent to children because they are already part of their speaking vocabulary (Clark, 1992). Because structural analysis with morphemes is usually reserved for later elementary grades and middle school, teachers might want to teach the most common set mentioned above as word parts to use for decoding early in students' reading development, perhaps around second grade, and save analysis of morphemes as meaningful units for later, perhaps third grade and beyond, as children gain vocabulary experience.

Although prefixes like *re-* and *un-* and suffixes like *-ly* and *-ful* are also morphemes, it is important to realize that these spellings do not always function as morphemes in words. For example, *re-* is a morpheme in *remaster* but not in *really* or *read*. When these word parts are meaningful ("*Re-* means to do it again."), teachers can gain triple benefit by combining instruction in separating the morphemes (which assists students with decoding), understanding the meanings of morphemes (which assists with building listening and speaking vocabulary, as well as with reading vocabulary), and learning rules for combining morphemes with other word parts (which assists with spelling as well as with reading). Tables 7.1 and 7.2 show reasonable orders for introducing prefixes and suffixes, along with their meanings and a few examples of each in words. Notice that inflected endings (*-ed*, *-ing*, *-s*, *-es*) are not on this list because students generally learn them prior to learning these morphemes.

Although other prefixes and suffixes are also useful, the collection in Tables 7.1 and 7.2 accounts for more than 85% of the affixes in common words. As in teaching any new concept to students, many, many examples of words that use the affix and frequent review will be needed before students with reading difficulties easily recognize these parts of words and use the orthographic patterns and the meanings to enrich their understanding and usage of words. Teachers can use unabridged dictionaries as good sources for lists of words to study, along with *The Reading Teacher's Book of Lists* (Fry et al., 2000). Along with lists of words, students will need a gradual introduction to a few rules for combining word parts, which follows in the section on rule-based decoding later in this chapter.

TABLE 7.1. Prefixes for Second through Fifth Grades

Prefix	Meaning	Examples
un-, dis-, in-	not	uncoil, unaware, disloyal, dislike, invisible, incomplete
re-	again	redo, resurface
en-, em-	to make	enlarge, embolden
non-	not	nonsense, nonbinding
in-	in	inland, inlaid
mis-	wrong	misspell, misidentify
sub-	under	submarine, subzero
pre-	before	preschool, precaution
im-, ir-, il-	not	imperfect, irrelevant, illegal
inter-	between	interstate, interpersonal
fore-	before	foreshadow, forejudge
de-	negate, away from	degrease, declaw
trans-	across	transatlantic, transpolar
super-, out-, over-	excess	superman, supermarket, outperform, overflow
semi-	half	semicircle, semiliterate
anti-	against	anticlimax, antihero
mid-	in the middle	midnight, midpoint
bi-	two	bicolor, bicycle

TABLE 7.2. Suffixes for Second through Fifth Grades

Suffix	Meaning	Examples
-er, -or	one who, something that	worker, teacher, computer, heater
-ly	in the manner of (creates an adverb)	friendly, gladly
-ful	full of	wonderful, spiteful
-ness	with	kindness, happiness
-less	without	matchless, childless
-tion, -sion	create the noun form	construction, subtraction, television, repression
-ment	creates the noun form	government, enjoyment
-able, -ible	able to, adjective	dependable, visible
-al	forms nouns from verbs	refusal, denial
-y	inclined to be (creates an adjective)	funny, juicy
-ity	creates the noun form	equality, electricity
-ive	creates adjective	decisive, expressive
-en	creates an adjective	oaken, golden
-ent, -ant	creates noun or adjective	pleasant, attendant, different, president
-ous	full of	adventurous, nervous
-ian, -ist	one who studies	librarian, historian, colorist, violinist

Identifying Syllables and Syllable Types

Not all multisyllabic words have the affixes described above. In addition to words with the *-le* ending (*middle, baffle*), students need to recognize that each syllable will have at least one vowel letter. By demonstrating how to locate the vowels in a long word (for example, in words like *mistletoe* or *concentrate*), students can learn to predict the number of syllables the word contains and where the breaks might fall. This process is shown below.

The teacher writes the following words on the board:

evident

sustainable

anticipating

population

denominator

TEACHER	STUDENTS
Let's clap the syllables in a few long words. Clap *probable*.	*Pro-ba-ble.*
How many syllables?	Three.
Clap *probability*.	*Pro-ba-bil-i-ty.*
How many syllables?	Five.
When you see a word that you don't know, it would help to read it if you could predict how many syllables it had, just by looking at it. Here's how to do that: Every syllable has at least one vowel. Say that rule: Every syllable has at least one vowel.	Every syllable has at least one vowel.
Let's look at this word. (*Points to* evident.) Where are the vowels? (*Underlines the vowels in* evident *as the students read them off.*)	*E - i - e.*
OK. Three vowels. Are any of the vowels teamed up?	No.
That's right, so probably each vowel represents a syllable. How many syllables are we looking for?	Three.
Let's look at where the vowels are: <u>E</u>v<u>i</u>d<u>e</u>nt. Where would you like to try to break up the three syllables?	*Ev-id-ent.*
Is that a word you've heard before?	It sounds like a word if you put *-dent* together. *Ev-i-dent. Evident.*

It's OK to play with where to break the word up. How many syllables in *evident*?

Ev-i-dent. Three.

Let's underline the vowels in this word. (*Points to* sustainable.)

U - a - i - a - e.

Any vowel teams here?

Ai.

Yes, we'll draw a line under that pair together, because it acts like one vowel when the team works together to make a sound.

U - ai - a - e. We know *able*, that's two syllables already.

Yes, so we can just look at this part. (*Covers* -able *so that students see only* sustain.) How many syllables in this part?

Two. *Sus-tain.*

Good. Put the word back together.

Sustainable.

Now, here's a long one. (*Points to* anticipating.) Find the vowels. (*Underlines the vowels as the students name them.*) Vowel teams?

A - i - i - a - i. No. And the last syllable's *-ing.* We know that one.

Yes, it ends in *-ing*, so we'll look at the rest of the word. How many more syllables?

Four more, plus *-ing.*

Where would you like to break it up?

An-ti-ci-pat-ing.

Fine. Read it again.

Anticipating.

(*Continues with the last words.*)

[Note that the teacher allows some exploration around where to break up the word, and—at least the first few times this activity is used—reminds students that vowel teams function as just one sound and, therefore, represent just one syllable.]

Few words separate syllables between two vowels, but many words use two consonants as dividers. For example, words like *picnic, basket, mascot,* and *perfect* all follow the pattern of vowel–consonant–consonant–vowel, and all divide syllables between the consonants. It is worthwhile to spend at least 1 week of instruction on words that separate the syllables between the consonants because these words are common in text materials for students in second and third grades, as words grow in length. When students can break this type of word at the syllable, each syllable becomes decodable.

To teach students to use the rule, show children lists of words that follow this pattern on several consecutive days. Sally Shaywitz presents such a list in her book *Overcoming Dyslexia* (2003, p. 216; see Table 7.3).

TABLE 7.3. Words That Divide between Consonants

absent	common	happen	napkin	success
attic	cotton	helmet	pencil	sudden
basket	custom	hidden	plastic	tablet
blanket	dentist	himself	possum	tennis
blossom	fallen	insect	problem	traffic
bottom	funnel	kidnap	public	triplet
button	gallop	kitten	puppet	trumpet
cactus	goblet	lesson	rabbit	tunnel
cannot	gossip	magnet	ribbon	upset
cobweb	gotten	mitten	signal	velvet

Note. Reprinted from *Overcoming Dyslexia* by Sally E. Shaywitz (Knopf, 2003). Copyright 2003 by Sally E. Shaywitz. Reprinted by permission.

Each day, ask students to underline the vowels in a list of words. This step of the procedure is useful for virtually all syllable types. Next, direct students to find the two consonants between the vowels. Ask them to draw a line between the consonants to divide the word. Then ask students to sound out each part and put the two parts back together to make the word.

Syllables that are bounded by consonants, like all of the examples above, are called closed syllables because the vowel is enclosed on each side by a consonant. Teaching students to recognize other syllable types can also be useful as students break apart long words. Barbara Wilson (1988) developed a reading program called the Wilson Reading System, in which students learn to recognize and take advantage of these syllable types to read long words. The Wilson Reading System has generated positive results for students in case studies, quasi-experimental studies, and in-school evaluations (Mather & Goldstein, 2001; O'Connor & Wilson, 1995). Other types of syllables include open (syllables that end in long vowels, such as in *na*tion and *be*long), vowel team (syllables where two or more letters create the vowel sound, such as in *eigh*t or *rai*n), consonant–*le* discussed earlier (as in mudd*le* or drizz*le*), r-controlled vowels (as in f*or*tune or m*ur*ky), and vowel–consonant–*e* (as in comp*ose* or reinst*ate*). Because each type of syllable will require considerable practice, each should be introduced and practiced over a few weeks of instruction, and each will need review as a new pattern is introduced. You will find the Wilson Reading System among the resources in Appendix A.

Complex Strategies: DISSECT and BEST

The generalizations described above are sometimes combined in words of two or more syllables, and so students will eventually need to learn strategies that allow flexible application of all they have learned so far. Two multistep research-based strategies that require students to break apart and analyze long words are DISSECT and BEST. DISSECT (Lenz & Hughes, 1990) was developed for middle school students and includes rules for where to break words (syllable types, described as the rule of twos and threes) and dictionary skills for students to use as back-up assistance. For students in the elementary school years, the BEST strategy (O'Connor & Bell, 2004; O'Connor et al., 2005) has been shown to be effective; it incorporates many of the same features found in DISSECT. BEST builds on students' knowledge of affixes and the vowels that signal syllables. To teach this strategy, teachers begin by showing students the acronym and teaching them to pair each letter of the strategy to a decoding action:

B = Break the word apart
E = Examine each part
S = Say each part
T = Try the whole thing in context

Memorizing the acronym and actions for each letter will take several minutes the first day and less time each day as students review the four parts and learn how to use the acronym. The first step—break the word apart—incorporates recognition and isolation of affixes, identification of a base word, and using vowels to separate syllables.

On the first day, include three or four words and guide each step of the strategy. For example, show students the word *expedition*. If affixes have been taught, then students will recognize *ex-* and *-tion*, and will break these parts away from the others. If they have been taught that each word part contains a vowel or vowel team, then that leaves *-pe-* and *-di-* as parts to examine. As they say each part, it is likely that students will generate a slowly pronounced version of the word that is very close to the correct pronunciation by the time they reach the final step.

In our research, students with reading disabilities understood the process after 4 or 5 days of instruction (about 5 minutes each day, with a new list of words), but it took another 2 weeks before we observed students challenging each other to BEST a long word that they encountered in their reading (O'Connor et al., 2005). Therefore, research experience would suggest that teachers should use this strategy with students for a few minutes daily for at least 3 weeks.

Generating Word Webs

As students learn a range of affixes, they will need practice recognizing them easily within words and determining how they influence a word's meaning. One effective way to practice variations based on morphemes is through word webs (Bos, Mather, Silver-Pacuilla, & Narr, 2000), in which children use a list of learned morphemes and group discussion to generate a range of potential variations around a base word. Children could start with a familiar word, such as *color*, and build inflected forms (*colors, colored, coloring*) and forms with different meanings by switching morphemes along with varying inflected forms (*recolor, recoloring, recolored, colorful, colorfulness, colorless, colorlessness, colorist, discolor, discolored*, etc.).

Students enjoy discovering how large they can build a small familiar word, and the practice makes it easier to unlock word parts in other words they may encounter when they do not have the support of the small-group brainstorming. This procedure is shown below.

TEACHER	STUDENTS
In the play we read, the bear had to identify his own bowl and chair. Let's look at that word. (*Writes* identify *on the board.*) What does *identify* mean?	He had to pick out which ones were his.
Yes. Now, are there endings or affixes you could add to *identify* to make it a longer word?	*Identified.* *Identifying.*
(*As students call out possibilities, adds them to the board to build a word web of the base words and legal affixes.*)	*Identity* is close to *identify*. Do those words fit together?
I'll add *identity* down here with a question mark and we'll look that word up. They might be related words. What else?	*Misidentify.*
What would *misidentify* mean? Good, we'll add it here. Other forms of *misidentify*?	Identify it wrong.

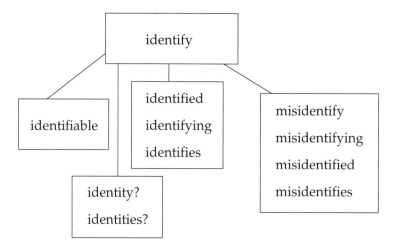

Last, the teacher leads the students through reading each cluster of words they created. By expanding on forms of a word, students gain experience adding and removing affixes, which will help them read and spell words.

RULE-BASED DECODING FOR WORDS WITH ENDINGS

Spelling manuals are often criticized for introducing too many rules that are found seldom in the words children see every day. Nevertheless, some spelling rules are necessary for reading longer words effectively. These rules involve changes in the spellings of base words and include when to drop the silent *e* as endings are added to words, the effect of doubling a consonant before adding an ending, and how to recognize when a *y* has been changed to an *i*. Each of these rules informs students about what to expect of vowel sounds. They help with the pronunciation of words, along with students' ability to identify the word parts and morphemes.

Dropping the Silent -*e*

Children in first grade often learn that *e*'s are dropped in common words like *making* and *liked*, but they rarely learn to analyze why this occurs or how to determine whether to drop an -*e* in the words they write. The rule is simple and easy to teach, and when students follow it, they will usually be correct in their attempts to spell as well as read words with suffixes.

Teach students to drop the -*e* when the next part of the word begins with a vowel. If students are shown multiple examples of adding a range of suffixes to words that do or do not end in -*e*, they can learn to use the rule across a wide range of words. For example, rather than show a long list of words in which -*ing* is added, show students a mix of words and endings, as in Table 7.4.

For each word, ask, "Does the word end in -*e*? Does the next part begin with a vowel? So will you drop the -*e*?" (Dixon & Engelmann, 1980). Requiring students to reflect on what the rule means and how to apply it across a range of words and endings means they learn a strategy upon which they can rely as they examine long words.

Doubling a Consonant

The doubling rule is important because it signals the difference between long and short vowel sounds in words with suffixes. Students need to understand that when a consonant has been doubled, it preserves the short vowel sound. They also need to learn that the final consonant in a base word is only doubled when the base word ends in a consonant–vowel–consonant pattern and the suffix to be added begins with a vowel letter. Although that combination of conditions seems compli-

TABLE 7.4. A Sample List of Words for Teaching Students When to Drop the Final -*e* from a Base Word

make + ing	come + ly	arrange + ment
sleep + less	preside + ent	arrange + ed
flute + s	age + less	close + ly
please + ing	late + est	televise + ion
please + ed	govern + ment	treat + able
state + ment	sense + ible	cure + able

cated, using the rule usually generates a correct spelling of these words, as well as assisting with reading the words. Students can be taught to look for this pattern. Dixon and Engelmann (1980) explain the rule to students through these steps:

> Does the word end in consonant–vowel–consonant (CVC)?
> Does the next part begin with a vowel?
> So will you double the final consonant?"

Couple these questions with a list of words each day in which students examine the base word and the endings and determine whether to double the final consonant (as examples, drip + ing, drip + less, stop + ed, prefer + ed, win + ing, wonder + ful, kind + ness, put + ing, sad + ness). After students learn the rule thoroughly, which will take several days of instruction and practice, students can examine lists of multisyllabic words to determine where this rule has been applied. Instruction for the doubling rule follows.

The teacher writes these words in columns on the board:

run	ing	spin	er
flat	ly	seed	less
horse	s	slip	er
strap	ing	buy	ing
strap	less	fast	est

TEACHER	STUDENTS
Today we're going to learn when to double the consonant in a word before adding an ending. Here's the rule: When the word ends in CVC and the next part begins with a vowel, you double the consonant. Say it with me: When the word ends in CVC and the next part begins with a vowel, you double the consonant.	When the word ends in CVC and the next part begins with a vowel, you double the consonant.
Say it with me again: When the word ends in CVC (*pauses for students to repeat*) and the next part begins with a vowel (*pauses*) you double the consonant. (*As students say the rule, touches under the last three letters in the base word. Rehearses the rule until students say it correctly.*)	When the word ends in CVC and the next part begins with a vowel, you double the consonant.
Here's how it works. (*Points to* run.) Does the word end in CVC? (*Underlines the three letters so that children can evaluate it for the consonant–vowel–consonant pattern.*)	Yes.

Does the next part (*points to* -ing) begin with a vowel?	Yes.
So will you double the final consonant? (*Points to the* n *in* run.)	Yes.
Let's write *running*. (*Writes it.*)	(*Write* running.)
When do you double the final consonant? (*If students cannot say the rule, rehearses it with them as before.*)	When the word ends in CVC and the next part begins with a vowel, you double the consonant.
(*Underlines the last three letters in* flat.) Does *flat* end in CVC?	Yes.
(*Points to* -ly.) Does the next part begin with a vowel?	No.
So will you double the final consonant? (*Points to the* t *in* flat.)	No.
Write *flatly*.	(*Write* flatly.)
Why didn't you double the *t*?	Because the next part doesn't start with a vowel.
When do you double the final consonant? (*If students cannot say the rule, rehearse, it with them as before.*)	When the word ends in CVC and the next part begins with a vowel, you double the consonant.

(*Works through the remaining examples with the students.*)

[If students make errors, refer them to the rule and have them work out the correct spelling by following the rule.]

Changing *y* to *i*

The final -*y* in a base word is usually changed to an *i* before adding an ending, unless the word ends in -*ey* or you are adding -*ing*. Thus, *happy* + *ness* becomes *happiness*, *marry* + *ed* becomes *married*, but *marry* + *ing* becomes *marrying* and *journey* + *s* becomes *journeys*. To teach this rule, be sure to include base words that end in -*y* and -*ey* and endings that begin with vowels and consonants, so that students do not overgeneralize what they learned from dropping the -*e* before adding suffixes. Also include in the list each day a few -*ing* endings so that students learn when not to change the *y* to an *i*. A procedure for teaching plural forms of words that end in -*y* is shown below.

TEACHER	STUDENTS
We're going to learn how to read and spell the plural forms of words that end in *-y*. Here's the rule: If the word ends in consonant-*y*, change the *y* to *i*, and add *-es*. Say it with me: If the word ends in consonant-*y*, change the *y* to *i*, and add *-es*. (*Teacher and students rehearse the rule a few times until students can say it without the teacher's assistance.*)	If the word ends in consonant *y*, change the *y* to *i*, and add *-es*.
(*Writes* city *on the board.*) Does *city* end in consonant-*y*?	Yes.
How will you write *cities*?	Change the *y* to *i* and add *-es*.
Yes. Write *cities*.	(*Write.*)
Look at *boy*. (*Writes* boy *on the board.*) Does boy end in consonant-*y*?	No.
So you don't change the spelling. Write *boys*.	(*Write.*)
Why didn't you change the spelling?	*Boy* doesn't end in consonant-*y*.
Say the rule.	If the word ends in consonant-*y*, change the *y* to *i*, and add *-es*.
(*Continues with these examples:* sky, play, guy, country, monkey, beauty. *Each time the teacher asks students if the word ends in consonant-*y* to prompt the correct spelling of the word. When students have completed writing all the plurals, she has the group of students read their plural forms and discuss which y's they changed and why.*)	
[If students spell a word incorrectly, refer them to the rule.]	

The feature of retaining the spelling of words that end in vowel-*y* also applies when adding endings that are not plurals. When students have thoroughly learned the plural forms above, they will be ready to add other kinds of suffixes. The procedure below shows how this might be accomplished.

TEACHER	STUDENTS
Think of the rule for changing words that end in *y* into plurals. Say that rule.	If the word ends in consonant-*y*, change the *y* to *i*, and add *-es*.

Exactly. For most endings that we add to words that
end in consonant-*y*, we change the *y* to *i* before we add
that ending. The exception is endings that start with *i*,
like *-ing* or *-ish*. That would give us a double *i*, which
almost never occurs in English words. Let's look at
some examples. (*Writes these words and endings in
columns on the board*):

Base words	Base words	Endings
lovely	journey	-est
boy	heavy	-ness
silly	play	-ish
reply	beauty	-ing
		-ed
		-ful

Does lovely end in consonant-*y*?	Yes.
We want to add *-est*. Will we change the *y* to *i*? Why? Write *loveliest*.	Yes. We're not adding another *i*. (*Write and check.*)
What if we wanted to write *loveliness*?	You'd still change the *y* to *i*.
Write *loveliness*.	(*Write and check.*)
Does *boy* end in consonant-*y*?	No.
Write *boyish*.	(*Write* boyish *and point out that they wouldn't change the* y *anyway because they're adding* -ish.)
Will you change the *y* to *i* to write *silliness*?	Yes.
Good. Write *silliness*.	(*Write and check.*)

(*Continues to direct students through writing* replied,
replying, journeyed, heaviest, heaviness, playful,
beautiful. *Calls on students to read some of the words
they wrote, and to justify why they did or did not
change the* y *to* i.)

[If students misspell words, direct them to the
rule and ask them to change their spelling.]

Along the way, students inevitably bring up the word *skiing*, which can open
an interesting question about whether this word actually breaks the rule. Since ski
doesn't end in *-y*, students learn that *skiing* is not only one of the rare words with

double *i*, but also has nothing to do with the rule. On one hand, these rules for changing a *y* to an *i* are clearly spelling rules. On the other hand, when students understand the function of the *i* before an ending, it helps them to break long words apart and to regenerate the base word (e.g., to change *silli + ness* to *silly + ness*), which is clearly a reading skill. That is why in the instructional routines above, teachers ask students to read back the words that they have spelled.

Students who falter in their reading development at the stage of reading multisyllabic words need a range of flexible strategies. These strategies involve thoughtful word analysis, rather than simple memorization of lists. All of these strategies require structured teaching in the early phases as students learn the steps and how to apply them to unfamiliar words. The research reviewed in this chapter reveals many effective strategies to teach long words, but teachers should realize that each new method requires instruction that spans several sessions per week over many weeks before students will be able to use these strategies independently and reliably.

CHAPTER 8

Reading Words Fluently

Although reading words accurately is an important reading milestone, it may not be sufficient to ensure that students read fluently—that is, read smoothly and effortlessly with appropriate rate and phrasing. Without fluency, comprehension of passages may be impeded. Theoretically, students who recognize words effortlessly should be able to devote more attention to reading comprehension (Laberge & Samuels, 1974; Perfetti, 1985), and the relationship between rate of oral reading and reading comprehension is strong through the elementary years (Pinnell et al., 1995).

Slow and labored reading is a hallmark of reading disability. With increased practice and repeated exposure to the words in texts, word recognition should become increasingly automatic. There is ample evidence that one of the major differences between good and poor readers is the amount of time they spend reading. Unfortunately, in observations in classrooms Allington (1977) and Biemiller (1977–78) found that the students who needed the most practice in reading spent the least amount of time actually reading. Researchers have reported that good readers are exposed to anywhere from 2 to 10 times as many words as poor readers (Adams, 1990). This difference is partly due to reading practice in school, but better readers also choose to read more in and outside of school because reading is easy and they enjoy it. We do not know which is antecedent and which is consequence—if independent reading practice contributes to reading achievement or if reading achievement enables and encourages independent reading.

Decoding practice by itself, although it improves word recognition, does not necessarily improve reading rate (Torgesen, Rashotte, & Wagner, 1997). Researchers have attempted to tease out the best ways to achieve this automatic word recognition. Studies in which students learned to recognize words quickly in lists have produced inconsistent findings for fluency in context. Fleischer, Jenkins, and Pany (1979) found few improvements in reading comprehension for teaching children to recognize words quickly out of context. Levy, Abello, and Lysynchuk (1997) taught children to recognize words faster using a combination of articulatory awareness and manipulating letters and sounds within syllables (much like the strategies in Chapters 4 and 5). This kind of instruction yielded faster reading of individual words, and many students transferred improved rate to oral reading of connected text. Nevertheless, the researchers found that students' reading comprehension did not improve unless students recognized the words nearly as quickly in context as in lists. The range of reading speed among their participants led these researchers to suggest that most students with reading difficulties would need considerable practice before they were likely to generalize to improved reading fluency in stories and books.

So, despite the importance of accurate reading of words, research has found an additional edge for students who can read words quickly. The relationship between fluent reading and reading comprehension has been very strong in most studies (O'Connor et al., 2002; Rupley, Willson, & Nichols, 1998; Spear-Swerling & Sternberg, 1994), with correlations in the range of .6 to .9. In fact, when the ability to read words and the rate of reading are measured concurrently, reading rate contributes significantly to reading comprehension even after the ability to read words accurately in lists has been accounted for (Jenkins et al., 2003; Schatschneider, 2004).

It must be clear by now that rate and fluency of reading is one piece of the reading comprehension puzzle, and yet the National Reading Panel (2000) found fewer experimental studies about reading fluency than any other single aspect of children's reading. Part of the problem for researchers is that improving fluency takes extensive practice, generally spanning half a year or more. In this chapter, I review what is known about reading fluency interventions and how teachers can improve the rate at which their students read words in running text.

RESEARCH ON IMPROVING READING RATE

How can teachers encourage the extensive practice needed to improve fluency? One of the most promising approaches is repeated reading. In repeated reading, students read a passage or page of text several times until improvement in the rate of reading (usually 25% increase or more) is achieved (Samuels, 1979). Herman (1985) found that repeated reading not only increased rate, but also accuracy of word recognition. Young, Bowers, and MacKinnon (1996) also found improvement in word recognition through repeated reading but only when students were assisted with their errors during practice. This distinction is important because some models of repeated reading have found that students can achieve rate improvements by rereading text independently or along with tape-recorded text.

When the goal is to improve accuracy of reading words along with rate, assistance from a more skilled reader—adult or peer—may be necessary.

In a review of the repeated reading literature, Meyer and Felton (1999) provided procedures for implementing fluency practice, along with the results teachers can expect to achieve. They provided rate guidelines for words per minute (wpm) in grades 1 and 2 (30–50 wpm in grade 1, 85–100 wpm for grade 2; drawn from Mercer & Campbell, 1998), which are consistent with the research that relates rate of reading across grade levels with student scores on high-stakes tests in third grade (Good, Simmons, et al., 2001). These rate goals for repeated reading are generally higher than would be expected on unpracticed reading, particularly for students who read poorly.

Measuring reading rate requires listening to students read aloud. The upper limits of oral-reading fluency are determined by the speed of speech, generally 150–180 wpm. Although many students achieve their maximum oral-reading rate by third or fourth grade, students with disabilities or with poor reading achievement may continue to need fluency practice throughout the elementary grades. By the time students read 150 wpm or more, continuing fluency practice is probably not helpful. Because the reading fluency of struggling readers is related to their reading achievement levels, fluency practice should be continued until reading achievement reaches fourth grade level or beyond.

From reviews of comprehensive approaches to building fluency, several general recommendations are supported consistently across all approaches (Kuhn & Stahl, 2003; Mercer & Campbell, 1998; Wolf & Bowers, 1999). Students should (1) practice building fluency for 10–20 minutes per day over a long duration such as a school year, (2) engage in reading aloud (versus listening), and (3) use text at an instructional level. For students who have difficulty decoding words as well as reading them fluently, teachers should also incorporate phoneme segmentation and blending, opportunities to learn common orthographic patterns within words, and decoding strategies until these skills are learned thoroughly.

Recommended Reading Rates

Two recent longitudinal studies present converging evidence for reading rates that are appropriate and for reading rates that should be worrisome for teachers. Table 8.1 combines data from these studies (Good, Simmons, et al., 2001; O'Connor et al., 2005) to show average reading rates in grades 1–3 and rates to consider dangerous because students who read slower than these rates continued to struggle with reading through the fourth grade.

For teachers who monitor their students' reading rates in grade-level materials, these numbers show that average readers in second grade in December read about 75 wpm. Second graders who read fewer than 50 wpm in December are at risk for continuing reading difficulties unless their skills improve rapidly, which usually means that teachers will need to find ways to address the word recognition and fluency problems of these very slow readers.

TABLE 8.1. Reading Rates across Grades

Grade	Average rate	Danger rate
Grade 1, May	60	40
Grade 2, December	75	50
Grade 2, May	100	60
Grade 3, December	120	70
Grade 3, May	135	80

As of 2006, research studies have not supported reasons for pushing students to read much faster than 130 wpm aloud, even though good readers in fourth and fifth grade usually read faster than that. Moreover, some students with reading disabilities might achieve adequate reading comprehension at slower rates, say around 100 wpm. Eventually, it is likely that research on reading fluency will reveal optimal rates to stimulate comprehension, which is the purpose behind improving reading rate and fluency.

A Word about Silent Reading

One of the more surprising findings from the National Reading Panel (2000) was that no research support could be found for using silent reading practice as an intervention to improve fluency. This finding was troubling and confusing for teachers who have implemented silent reading as part of their daily routines for many years, with practices such as DEAR (Drop Everything and Read) and USSR (Uninterrupted Sustained Silent Reading). The reason that silent reading has minimal impact on the fluency of poor readers is revealed when we ask teachers to describe what their worst readers do during these 15- to 20-minute practice opportunities. Teachers rarely mention reading. More often, they describe students who listlessly turn pages or who find something else to do during this time—often something that gets them into trouble. Without feedback on their reading accuracy, some poor readers make too many mistakes as they read silently to gain skills or to become interested in the material they are reading.

Although silent reading has little impact on improving fluency, there are other reasons to encourage children who can read words to read silently, such as for enjoyment of reading, for finding information, and for exploring new vocabulary words. But as a fluency builder, methods that include a skilled listener to a child's reading are much more effective.

ACTIVITIES TO IMPROVE STUDENTS' READING RATE AND FLUENCY

In studies of students with reading disabilities, the difficulty of developing sufficient reading rate to enable comprehension figures prominently. Several methods for increasing reading fluency have been tested in classroom settings. Methods for working with students one-on-one and for using class peers to improve fluency are described in this section.

Rereading

Researchers who study students reading aloud with adult assistance recommend reading text more than once because it provides students with multiple repetitions of the same words within a short time (Dowhower, 1987; 1991; Samuels, 1979; Shany & Biemiller, 1995; Sindelar et al., 1990). Redundancy of groups of words from one passage to another ranges around 40–53% in second- and third-grade-level materials (O'Connor et al., 2002), and this redundancy is especially beneficial for struggling readers. Mathes and Fuchs (1993) found that students benefited as much from practicing with instructional-level text (accuracy around 90–95%) as with independent reading-level text (accuracy around 98%), but evidence suggests few benefits when the reading levels of practice materials are far above students' reading level (O'Connor et al., 2002).

Rereading is a practice routine that pairs one student with an adult listener. The procedure takes about 10 minutes per session and should be used at least three times per week to generate significant improvement in fluency. To use this strategy, teachers:

- Select passages of 100–200 words near the students' current reading level.
- Time the student's first reading of the passage and record the time.
- Direct students to reread the passage until they can read with 95% accuracy in 75% of the time it took for the first reading (usually three or four readings).
- Record the number of rereadings to achieve the goal.

For the next practice session, teachers select a new 100- to 200-word passage and repeat the procedure. Over time, fluency improves, probably due to the redundancy of words across passages at a particular reading level. Roughly half the words students learn to recognize quickly during the rereading of one passage will be seen again in succeeding passages on future days, and these words will be recognized more quickly in the next passage.

Teachers sometimes wonder when they will have the time to use a strategy like rereading, regardless of its benefits. One possibility is to use the rereading procedure with a struggling reader during the time that good readers are reading silently. It is likely that the 20 minutes of silent reading was wasted for this student previously, and it provides an available time for teachers to promote fluency with one or two poor readers while other students are occupied usefully.

Partner Reading

Rereading one-on-one with a student and adult listener can be difficult to manage with a large class, but partner reading is much easier to organize. Teachers have often paired students to practice reading or to finish a chapter, but this method does not always work effectively unless teachers arrange these opportunities carefully.

Imagine this scenario: Ms. O wants her students to read well, and knows that several students in her class are slow readers. One student in particular—Mark—is very slow and often makes mistakes. She thinks about her students and selects a partner for Mark who is bound to be helpful. Tim is an excellent reader, and also a model class citizen who is kind, nearly always on task, and likes Mark. She pairs Mark and Tim and assigns all pairs of readers in her class to read pages 37–45. She explains that they are to read one page each, and trade turns reading the section aloud. When they are finished, they can select a game to play on one of the class computers.

Tim reads the first page as Mark listens, and then Mark begins to read. His reading is slow, even painful to listen to but Tim is helpful and kind and assists him with the hard words so that Mark eventually gets through his page of text. Tim reads again; Mark listens, then reads when it is his turn. Tim continues to be helpful but begins to notice that his classmates are finishing the assignment and moving onto the computers, where they appear to be having quite a good time. By the time this pair finishes the assigned reading, the class is lining up for recess. Ms. O has monitored the pair and is relieved to see how well the two boys worked together. So well, in fact, that she will assign them to work together again tomorrow.

The next day, when she assigns new pages to these partners, Tim pulls a face that dismays Mark. Although Tim wants to be helpful, he feels disheartened to miss out on computer games every day because he gets "stuck" with Mark and his slow reading rate. As the days wear on, he is less helpful, and, eventually, as Mark begins to read, Tim says, "Just listen. I'll read it," and reads the rest of the pages aloud to Mark. Mark listens, but he does not read along because he cannot keep up with the rapid pace. Because he has listened to the material, he will be able to participate in the discussion of the pages, but he received no practice at all in reading and no opportunity to improve his reading rate or fluency.

We see this scenario over and over again in classrooms that use partner reading (O'Connor & Jenkins, 1995), but there are better ways to organize this procedure in classrooms. Two methods of partner reading have received extensive research focus, and both have generated dramatic improvements in reading fluency (Greenwood, Delquadri, & Hall, 1989; Mcmaster, Fuchs, & Fuchs, 2006). These methods share two organizational secrets for making partner reading work in classrooms: (1) They are organized by *time* rather than pages of text (which means that all student pairs—with and without reading difficulties—finish at the same time), and (2) they require students to read the text at least *twice* (which engenders some of the benefits of repeated reading).

To ensure that all students have an equivalent amount of time practicing their reading, the teacher decides how much time to devote to reading fluency practice, perhaps 10 or 15 minutes 4 days each week. Depending on the method selected, the teacher pairs students into dyads with a higher and lower reader or into pairs with roughly equivalent reading ability. He or she sets a timer for half the allotted time, and the pairs read in the chosen method. When the timer sounds, students return to the beginning of the text and reread the same material. The sections below describe variations on time-controlled partner reading methods and provide more detail on using these methods.

Classwide Peer Tutoring

Classwide Peer Tutoring (CWPT), which was developed by Delquadri, Greenwood, and their colleagues at the Juniper Gardens Children's Project in Kansas City (Delquadri, Greenwood, Stretton, & Hall, 1983; Greenwood, Maheady, & Dequadri, 2002), promotes improved engagement and learning for students with disabilities and students with other academic difficulties in general education classes. CWPT has been used to develop students' skills in reading, spelling, and mathematics, but here I describe how to implement this approach to build reading fluency. The premises behind the approach are that students will benefit from more opportunity to practice important skills and that effective practice requires a high rate of responding. Contrast this method to a more traditional round-robin approach to reading aloud, and it becomes immediately apparent that students who participate in CWPT will have much higher rates of on-task behavior, in addition to much more opportunity to practice reading aloud.

In this method, all students in a class are paired to provide reciprocal support, and all class members act as both tutors and tutees within the same CWPT session. One student is the tutor as his or her partner reads aloud; halfway through the session, these roles switch. Each pair of readers is assigned to a team, and points are awarded during the session for appropriate behaviors, which include following along while the partner is reading, reading entire sentences correctly, and correcting errors as they occur.

As described in the Division for Learning Disabilities' Current Practice Alerts (Council for Exceptional Children, 2003), each week partners draw a red or blue piece of paper from a covered container to determine which team they will belong to during that week. Thus, throughout the week they are working to accrue points for themselves but also for the class team to which they belong. The standard protocol for awarding points in CWPT is for the tutor to award 2 points for correctly read sentences and 1 point for correcting an error (for example, the tutor provides the correct word, and the tutee goes back to the beginning of that sentence and reads the word correctly in the sentence for 1 point). The points the pairs accrue are added up each day and recorded on a team chart. Rewards for the winning team at the end of the week can be as easy as a class cheer, first team to line up for recess, or something more tangible at the teacher's discretion.

In a 4-year longitudinal study of students in socioeconomically low schools, Greenwood and colleagues (1989) found substantial positive effects of CWPT on standardized measures of reading comprehension and on reading fluency. They attribute the positive effects to more time engaged in reading aloud, better behavior from the low-skilled students, and the correction of errors by peers that enabled poor readers to comprehend the sentences they read.

Modeled Reading: Peer Assisted Learning Strategies

The Peer Assisted Learning Strategies (PALS) model for building reading fluency (Fuchs, Fuchs, Mathes, & Simmons, 1997; Fuchs et al., 2001) is a variation of CWPT. The activities described here to promote fluency are part of a longer reading session that includes practice on reading words, reading aloud to build fluency, and retelling the passage to activate reading comprehension. PALS incorporates many features of CWPT described above. Before pairing students, the teacher conducts a few minutes of word study with the reading group to prepare the students for new words in the reading material. For the fluency portion of PALS, the teacher pairs a higher- and lower-level reader and provides text that the poor reader can read with 90% accuracy or higher. The teacher sets a timer for a little less than half of the allotted reading time. For example, if 12 minutes has been allotted, the teacher may set the timer for 5 minutes.

The higher reader always reads first to provide a model for the less-skilled reader. While the higher reader reads the text, the less-skilled reader follows along. The teacher may provide a bookmark to make it easier to monitor students' reading along behavior. When the timer sounds, the lower-skilled reader reads the same piece of text with the higher-skilled reader acting as a coach and helping with hard words and general encouragement to keep reading until the timer sounds again. Recently, the researchers have modified the extended reading of the coach. Instead of reading for 5 uninterrupted minutes, the higher reader reads just one page, followed by the lower reader rereading that page. As before, the higher reader provides a model of fluent reading, exposure to difficult words, and a sense of the flow of the story, which helps the less-skilled reader to comprehend a passage prior to that student's turn to read it.

At the close of the reading fluency practice, students take 30 seconds to retell what they recall of the story, with the higher-skilled student retelling first. Other recent modifications to PALS include a speed game in which the less-skilled reader has two or more additional opportunities to reread a page of text with the higher-skilled reader keeping track of the time it takes to read the page. The point of the game is to beat the previous time, which echoes a major tenet of the rereading procedures suggested by Herman (1985), Dowhower (1987) and Sindelar et al. (1990).

A description of teacher and student activities during 15 minutes of fluency practice is shown below. The text used by this pair of readers is *Lions of the Plains* (Miranda, 1998), and they are following the page-by-page model of partner reading from PALS.

The teacher sets the timer for 14 minutes.

BETTER READER	STRUGGLING READER
OK. I'll read the first page. Are you ready?	Yep. (*Points to the first word on the page.*)
(*Begins to read aloud.*) The female lion left the others sleeping on the plain. She walked south to the hills. She scouted for a cave in a mound of rocks. The female lion found a good place to make her den. Then she dug out the ground to make a bed . . . (*Reads aloud until the end of the page.*)	(*Follows along by using a bookmark under each line of text.*)
OK, your turn. (*Follows along as the struggling reader reads.*) (*Points to the word* plain.) That word is *plain.*	(*Begins to read the same page.*) The female lion left the others sleeping on the path. She . . . Plain. The female lion left the others sleeping on the plain. She walked
Good!	(*hesitation*) south to the hills. She (*hesitation*) searched?
Scouted.	Scouted. She scouted for a cave in a mound of rocks. The female lion found a good place to make her den. Then she dug out the ground to make
(*Continues to assist with difficult words.*)	a bed . . . (*Reads to the end of the page.*)

At the beginning of the next page the better reader reads first again to model fluent reading. They continue through the text page by page, with the better reader always reading the page first. When the teacher's timer sounds, they stop reading. The teacher sets the timer for 30 seconds and announces, "Now it is time to retell the story. You may begin."

BETTER READER	STRUGGLING READER
OK, here's what I remember. The mother lion left the pride and went to a den to have her cubs. One had stripes and the other one didn't. She licked the cubs so they'd have her smell, and then she took a nap. They stayed there for a few weeks. (*The timer beeps.*)	(*Listens until the teacher's timer goes off in 30 seconds.*)

The teacher sets the timer for another 30 seconds and announces, "Now it is time to tell what else you remember. You may begin."

BETTER READER   STRUGGLING READER

There were two cubs. They were a
male and female. And their heads
were round. They couldn't walk at
first and they slept all the time. Or
most of the time. (*The timer goes off.*) So
we're done.

Teach Students to Use the Model

Students will need to receive training in any model of peer-assisted partner reading
in order to conduct their roles appropriately. One effective way to provide this
training is for a teacher to select a student to act as the teacher's partner so that they
can demonstrate to the class for 2 minutes how to listen to the tutee, how to correct
errors as they occur, how to provide encouragement, and how to record points if
they are used. After a 2-minute model with the teacher acting as tutor, the teacher
explains what his or her role as the tutor entails, asks the class for questions to be
sure this role is clear, and then switches roles with the student and demonstrates
for another minute or two how to conduct the role of the reader. Following another
brief discussion, the teacher can assign pairs and have partners engage in a mini-
practice session (no more than 2 minutes per role).

The teacher follows this practice with another brief discussion to clarify any
questions students may have about how much to read (Until the timer beeps? One
page at a time? Sentence by sentence?), how to correct a partner's errors (usually
just have tutors provide the word if they can—teaching word analysis is the
teacher's job), how to record points if the teacher decides to use points, and what to
do when it is time to switch roles.

Other Considerations in Partner Reading

In my observations in classrooms, I note that students who are poor readers are
often less engaged in instruction and less attentive as their partner is reading
aloud. For example, in the model of partner reading in which the first reader reads
for 5 minutes, the time span may be too long for the low-skilled reader to follow
along. It is this problem that the PALS developers addressed by limiting turns to
one page at a time. We have found further improvements in behavior by having
students read only one sentence at a time (O'Connor et al., 2005). Using this model
of partner reading, the teacher sets the timer for half of the allotted time. One student reads the first sentence, the partner reads the second sentence, and the two
continue back and forth, each reading one sentence and continuing through the
passage until the timer sounds. Then the partners return to the beginning of the
passage and switch roles so that the first reader becomes the second reader. By
switching who starts first, the passage is read a second time with each student

reading unique sentences that he or she did not read aloud before. This method is shown below. The students are reading *The Secret Soldier* by Ann McGovern (1975).

The teacher sets the timer for 7 minutes and says, "You may begin reading where you left off yesterday."

STUDENT	STUDENT
Here's the place. Do you want to start?	OK. (*Begins reading.*) Year by year, the United States was growing closer to the time when it could stand alone.
And year by year, Deborah was growing closer to her . . .	Can we BEST that word?

The pair breaks off the *in-* at the beginning and the *-ence* at the end. They recognize *depend* and put the word parts together.

STUDENT	STUDENT
Independence!	Independence!
Deborah was growing closer to her independence too—the time she could go out into the world and be on her own.	
	At last Deborah was 18 years old.
It was the year 1778 and she was free!	
	But free to do what?
She was a woman.	
	That meant she could not learn a trade, the way young men did.

The pair continues moving through the text, each reading one sentence until the timer beeps. The teacher then sets the timer for another 7 minutes and says, "Go back to the beginning and start when you're ready."

STUDENT	STUDENT
OK. My turn. Year by year, the United States was growing closer to the time when it could stand alone.	
	And year by year, Deborah was growing closer to her independence too—the time she could go out into the world and be on her own.
At last Deborah was 18 years old.	
	It was the year 1778 and she was free!

The pair continues to read until the timer beeps again, signaling the end of the partner reading period.

As in other models, the teacher can add 30 seconds of retelling time for each student to focus the pair on the content of what they read. It is likely that when students return to the beginning of the passage and read for the same amount of time, they will read a little farther in the text because of the practice the first time through.

We have found that attentional behavior increases dramatically when students read just one sentence in a turn because it is always "almost your turn" for the distractible student, and so the amount of time that students are engaged appropriately increases. When we use this sentence-by-sentence approach with older students who sometimes complain when they are asked to read a passage a second time, teachers respond, "But you didn't read *those* sentences" (because they are reading the ones that their partner read the first time), which usually forestalls the complaint.

The variations on partner reading described here have each been validated in controlled studies. Some teachers prefer having students read one page at a time (with the partner then rereading that page) because they believe that comprehension is preserved by reading larger chunks of text. Other teachers prefer the sentence-by-sentence variation because they believe it improves the behavior and attention of lower-skilled students as they practice reading for fluency.

These variations have not been tested against each other, so currently there are no grounds for recommending one approach over another, except to reiterate the importance of controlling partner reading by time instead of requiring students to complete a particular number of pages. By controlling for time, all students receive equivalent practice opportunity, and higher-skilled students are not punished for being paired with a lower-skilled student because all of the partner pairs finish at the same time.

Controlling the Difficulty Level of the Text

Recent evidence suggests that students who practice reading aloud in material that is too difficult (for example, a year or more above students' reading level) make minimal fluency improvements, even when they practice for several months (O'Connor et al., 2002). It is likely that students' mistakes will be so numerous that they will lose the sense and flow of what they are reading. Also, if students have not learned to recognize the words that recur most frequently at a particular level of text (because the text is too difficult), they may be sounding out most of the words and have little opportunity to begin to recognize words more quickly. Another advantage of managing partner reading with a set amount of time for all students to be reading is that teachers can use different text materials for different partner pairs. Even though several different levels of reading materials can be used, teachers can still conduct partner reading as a whole-class activity or as a pair-practice activity while the teacher works with another reading group.

When all students are reading at the same time, teachers can give each pair of students a story that is at their current reading level. For example, two pairs can be reading *Charlotte's Web*, two pairs *The Mouse and the Motorcycle*, and two pairs *Frog and Toad Are Friends*. Each pair reads a book at an appropriate reading level, and all students practice concurrently. Students receive the practice they need at the level that is best for them, and teachers find it easy to manage the fluency practice.

Monitoring Growth in Reading Rate

Teachers can monitor growth in the rate of students' reading periodically using oral-reading-rate measures, such as the Dynamic Indicators of Basic Early Literacy Skills (DIBELS) or the Test of Reading Fluency (TORF). Alternatively, teachers can assess rate and accuracy in students' current reading material by incorporating a 1-minute oral reading timing every week or two into the time set aside for partner reading. The purpose of using students' current reading material rather than a more generic set of grade-level passages is so that teachers can determine whether the material is too easy or too difficult.

To monitor rate and accuracy in the students' current material, the teacher listens to two or three pairs in turn during each fluency practice session and times students individually as they read a "cold" (unpracticed) passage in their book. She sits with one pair of students, points to the first word of a sentence and says, "Start when you are ready." She starts her stopwatch as the student begins to read, and keeps track of the number of errors with tick marks. When the student has read for 1 minute, she notes the last word read, and together they count the number of words the student read aloud. She notes that number, subtracts the number of errors, and records the number of words read correctly over the number of errors (e.g., 86/5). To determine the accuracy, she forms a ratio of the words read correctly (86 words) over the total number of words attempted (86 + 5, or 91) and generates an accuracy percentage (94.5%).

An example of a section of a class chart is shown in Figure 8.1, and a reproducible form is included in Appendix B. When students drop below 90% accuracy consistently, the teacher knows the material is too difficult. She was considering changing Carlos's level of reading material, but in the last two measures he improved, so she will watch to see if he stays above 90% over the next few measures. She could find an easier text for the pair of students or regroup students so that the difficulty level is appropriate. Note that this teacher has students reading a range of materials. Because she controls the partner reading by time, it is easy for her to manage several different difficulty levels of materials during the same instructional block of time.

Controlling for Noise

A final consideration merits attention: noise in the classroom during fluency practice. Any method will need to be modeled for the students before they try to use it

Students and Text and Date	1/12	1/26	2/9	2/23	3/9	3/23				
Hanin *Treasure Island*	70/3	72/3	85/4	85/3						
Sherise *Treasure Island*	97/0	92/1	76/2	99/2						
Paul *20,000 Leagues*	82/3	80/4	87/2	88/3						
Jazmine *20,000 Leagues*	72/3	59/2	74/2	80/2						
Angel *Frog and Toad*	48/4	55/2	50/5	52/4						
Carlos *Frog and Toad*	44/6	54/7	53/5	54/4						
James *Shackleton*	66/5	72/6	73/5	79/4						
Robin *Shackleton*	88/3	87/2	92/3	95/2						

FIGURE 8.1. Example of a class chart for monitoring progress in reading accuracy.

independently. During the modeling phase when a teacher and a student act out the roles for each partner pair, the teacher should also point out and demonstrate the use of a "6-inch voice." This voice is the level of sound that can be heard by a partner 6 inches away, but not by a student 6 or 10 feet across the classroom. Wouldn't it be nice if we could install a 6-inch voice as the rule for cell phone users in airports?

In summary, reviewing and rehearsing word lists are useful techniques for improving word recognition, but research indicates that fluent reading can best be acquired by practicing reading in a meaningful context at an instructional level. Teachers should understand that attaining meaningful increases in fluency will require considerable practice.

CHAPTER 9

Older Students
with Reading Difficulties

Much of the research on reading words has been conducted with beginning readers, but the same problems persist with older poor readers who have not learned to read words easily in the early grades. Research evidence has validated taking a similar approach to reading instruction with older poor readers, and these studies have clearly shown that it is not too late to teach students to read words or to improve their rate of reading (Abbott & Berninger, 1999; Lovett, Lacerenza, & Borden, 2000; O'Connor et al., 2002; Torgesen et al., 2001).

Reading words is an area of special challenge for older students with reading difficulties, who may be caught in what Ehri and McCormick (1998) describe as the partial alphabetic stage of reading development. These students have learned the consonants and some of the vowel sounds, but they have not anchored this knowledge in ways that can be used to read words accurately. Because these students fail to process all letters within a word, they make frequent errors and substitutions of words with similar visual shapes or lengths. Without attending to all letter combinations within words, students cannot decode words, nor can they analogize to known sight words (Ehri & Robbins, 1992; McCandliss et al., 2003). They are denied access to self-teaching mechanisms, in which good readers successfully decode the words they encounter in their reading so many times that those words become part of their corpus of instantly recognized words (Share, 1995).

Unlike young poor readers who lack strategies for reading new words, older poor readers have struggled with reading for several years and so are likely to have incorporated faulty strategies into their repertoire of reading and writing tools. Because of their prolonged difficulty, it may be difficult to inspire motivation to try again. Despite these factors that adversely affect older poor readers, there are also strengths that can be marshaled on behalf of these students. For example, older poor readers already have at least a rudimentary knowledge about the academic structure of school tasks, literacy, and language, and their comprehension and vocabulary knowledge are likely to be better than that of younger students who read at similar levels (Rack et al., 1992). They may, then, be better able than younger readers to benefit from metacognitive strategies for reading and writing, such as reading by analogy to known words (Gaskins, et al., 1988), analysis of letter patterns that recur across words (Glass, 1973), or use of morphemes to read and spell words (Carlisle, 2004; Dixon & Engelmann, 1980).

It is important as we move into reading approaches for older students to mention that teachers are often counseled to match modality strength or learning style to specific elements of reading instruction, particularly for students with learning disabilities. Nevertheless, comprehensive reviews by researchers who assessed the effect of matching modality (e.g., Arter & Jenkins, 1979; Kavale & Forness, 1987) or matching learning styles to instruction (e.g., Good, Vollmer, Katz, & Chowdhri, 1993) have failed to show positive effects of such matching. Rather, these studies suggest that our most powerful and well-researched instructional models—which often address multiple modalities—are particularly important for students with the most severe reading difficulties.

EFFECTIVE APPROACHES FOR READING WORDS

Several recent studies have developed and tested effective instructional approaches for students in the upper elementary and middle school grades who have failed to master the early skills of decoding and phonemic awareness. These techniques are described below, and they consistently shatter the familiar adage that after the primary grades, decoding instruction is far less effective than it would have been earlier. Programs that are available commercially are listed in Appendix A.

The ABD's of Reading

Some time ago, Joanna Williams (1980) developed a "starting over" approach for students with reading disabilities from age 7 through 12. Her ABD's program (*Analysis, Blending,* and *Decoding*) began with auditory segmenting and blending, much like the strategies recommended in Chapters 2 through 4 of this book. The program included letter sounds and a controlled sequence of blending activities that began with two- and three-letter words and worked up to decoding words with two syllables. In one half-day of professional development, teachers learned to implement the program for 20-minute sessions. At the end of the implementation year, students in treated classes outperformed control students in word identification quite dramatically. The results of her research dispelled the notion that older students fail to thrive with a phonics approach to reading words.

Auditory Discrimination in Depth

It has long been known that students with reading difficulties have difficulty hearing the sounds in words. Thirty years ago, Lindamood and Lindamood (1975, 1984) developed Auditory Discrimination in Depth (ADD) to help students focus on mouth position as they learn how each sound feels as it is pronounced. Students begin by segmenting words and identifying the phoneme type by articulatory gestures and voicing. For example, the articulatory gestures for the letters *p* and *b* are "lip poppers," but they differ in voicing. Students learn to discriminate vowel sounds by mouth and tongue positions and to use articulation as a kinesthetic cue for decoding words. The program requires intensive teacher training and is designed to be used individually or in very small groups. Students use pictures and colored blocks to make the phonemes in words concrete. Lessons gradually incorporate spelling along with reading words. Several studies have found ADD to produce reliable gains in word identification for children with especially low skills (Brady, Fowler, Stone, & Winburg, 1994; Truch, 1994; Wise, Ring, & Olson, 2000). The current version of the program is called LiPS (the Lindamood Phonemic Sequencing Program; see Appendix A).

Although this approach was initially used with young children who had difficulty acquiring basic sounds and letter–sound correspondences, it has also been used effectively with older students, and for good reason. A recent meta-analysis by Swanson (1999) identified articulation and memory for phonemes as particularly difficult for students with learning disabilities. In an experiment similar to their work with first and second graders, Torgesen and colleagues (2001) provided 100 minutes of individual instruction daily for about 9 weeks (67.5 hours total) to third-, fourth-, and fifth-grade students with learning disabilities to test the effects of two word-recognition treatments—ADD and Embedded Phonics (EP). In the ADD approach, students spent 85% of their instructional time decoding and spelling words with an extensive focus on articulation of phonemes. The remaining 15% of the time, students learned sight words and read connected text. In EP, 50% of the time focused on direct instruction of word-level skills (20% on phonemic decoding and 30% on sight words and spelling) and 50% on meaningful activities around reading-connected text. Principles of reading instruction identified as effective for students with learning disabilities (see Swanson, 1999), such as segmenting and blending, guided practice, and systematic cueing of strategies were incorporated in both approaches.

Both treatments were found to be effective overall, with significant differences in word attack (nonsense words) and reading rate (fluency) that favored the ADD condition by the end of the treatment. Word-recognition outcomes did not differ. On average, students in both conditions gained one standard deviation on a test of word identification, and more than half of the students gained sufficient skill to enter the average range (standard scores of 90 or above). On follow-up tests 2 years later, the two groups did not differ, and gains made during treatment on word recognition and comprehension were maintained. For many students, scores continued to improve even after the programs were discontinued. The authors concluded that the ADD and EP approaches were equally effective in the long run, and that the key to these dramatic improvements was the intensive one-on-one instruction, with both methods offering heavy doses of phonemic and decoding instruction.

Analysis for Decoding Only

While Williams's (1980) approach began with individual letter sounds, in Glass's Analysis for Decoding Only teachers use short high-frequency words to teach students how to analyze letter patterns that occur across words. The program provides four sets of cards, with each card focusing on one pattern and each set increasingly difficult. Each card in a set contains a keyword that students probably already know (e.g., *day*) along with lists of sequentially more difficult words containing the same orthographic pattern on which to apply the new letter pattern (e.g., *lay, trays, layer, delay, Sundays, delaying, payment*).

During instruction, students are first shown a word that they recognize, such as *rain*. Teachers show students how to extract and use the *-ain* pattern ("Which letters spell /ain/?") to decode words like *strain, detaining, container*, and others. As the difficulty level in each set increases, students incorporate previously taught patterns as well as learning new ones. Students might apply a learned pattern (e.g., *-er*) as they learn the new pattern *-ev-* in words such as *ever, every, crevice, several, evident, nevertheless*, and *revolution*. As in most effective strategies for decoding, teachers require students to engage actively in the analysis by eliciting which letters in the word the students examine make particular sounds ("Which letters spell /ev/? What sound does *e* + *v* make?"). This program is only for decoding words, and no connected reading of text is included (see Appendix A).

The Read-by-Analogy Approach

Gaskins and colleagues (1988) developed another alternative approach to phonics for word recognition at the Benchmark School in Pennsylvania for students with reading disabilities. Like Glass's analysis, the Benchmark approach takes advantage of the fact that most students who read poorly in grade 3 and beyond have already learned a collection of high-frequency words. In the Benchmark approach, these high frequency words, also called keywords or glue words (many of which are already in the sight word collection of these students) become the targets for teacher-guided scrutiny. Because students learn to use the words they already know to decode what they don't know, the program is only appropriate for students who already have a little reading under their belts. Taking advantage of the common invariant spelling patterns of these words, students are taught to analyze the words for their letter patterns. They gradually build their core of decodable words through a read-by-analogy approach, in which they learn to analyze unknown words in light of familiar spelling patterns.

In the experimental classrooms, each week about five new glue words were introduced and rehearsed. A list of all 120 of these words can be found in the published results (Gaskins et al., 1988). Students were taught to compare and contrast letter patterns in these words with the letter patterns of other known and unknown words. Students used a metacognitive comparative process to break apart unknown words and sound them out by using larger decoding chunks than the letter-by-letter strategy of phonics approaches, often at the level of the syllable. Each word-analysis lesson lasted 45–60 minutes, and the teaching style required students to respond frequently to teacher questions and prompts. Part of each lesson also required students to talk through their strategies for decoding difficult words with peers and the teacher. As words were learned, they were posted on a word wall and used cumulatively as new words and patterns were introduced in successive weeks. This metacognitive method has not been effective for beginning readers who lack a core of sight words (Nation et al., 2001), but several studies have documented positive effects on word recognition for older students. It is important for teachers to recognize that this program focuses on word analysis and that reading fluency was still slow for students who participated in the program for 2 years.

COMBINATION APPROACHES AND READING PACKAGES

It must be clear by now that older poor readers need to learn some way to decode the words they do not instantly recognize. Is one way better than another? Lovett and Steinbach (1997) tested the effects of the Benchmark School's metacognitive strategy against direct, systematic letter-by-letter decoding (i.e., phonics) used across 35 hours of instruction with students with reading disabilities in second through sixth grades. In the phonological analysis and blending approach (PHAB), students learned letter–sound correspondences, blending sounds of letters in words, and segmenting using lessons extracted from DISTAR Reading Mastery I (Engelmann & Bruner, 1995; see Appendix A).

In the metacognitive word instructional strategies training (WIST), students learned multiple approaches for recognizing words that included phonics and read-by-analogy instruction that was similar to the Benchmark approach. Students began with letter-by-letter decoding and proceeded through analogizing to known words (based on the Benchmark program), breaking off affixes, and seeking known parts of words (like the BEST approach described in Chapter 7). PHAB and WIST both also included reading connected text, and both produced sizable effects in word identification and word attack. In the experimental trials, students were able to transfer the patterns in the taught words to untaught words with the same spelling patterns in both conditions. No age effects were found, suggesting that these strategies were as effective with older students as they were with poor readers in the primary grades.

Continuing this line of inquiry, Lovett, Lacerenza, Borden, Frijiters, et al. (2000) combined the two treatments in various orders to determine the most effective combination of PHAB and WIST instruction when used across 70 hours of instruction. The most effective combination for developing word-recognition skills (which they labeled PHAST: phonological and strategy training) began with phonemic awareness, letter sounds, and decoding of short words and proceeded through strategy training in which students learned to select among five procedures for word recognition: letter-by-letter decoding, reading by analogy (based on the Gaskins et al., 1988, keyword method), seeking the part of the word you know (much like BEST), attempting variable pronunciations, and peeling off affixes in multisyllabic words. Each phase of the program is described in Lovett, Lacerenza, and Borden (2000). This approach was sequenced across difficulty levels, and students were taught the skills they would need to use each strategy successfully. Unlike Torgesen and colleagues' (2001) one-on-one instruction, Lovett, Lacerenza, and Borden's experimental test was conducted in small groups of four, which may be more manageable in schools that have many students with word-reading difficulties.

Working one-to-one in another package intervention, O'Connor and colleagues (2002) delivered 36 hours of reading instruction in one of two treatments to third-, fourth-, and fifth-grade students in the bottom 25% of their class in reading, half of whom had a formal diagnosis of reading disability. They tested the effects of two treatments that only differed in the level of text the students used for reading practice, from which the word patterns that students studied during the tutorials were generated. One treatment used text at the student's instructional level, and the other used materials that were matched to students' grade level. Both treatments incorporated about 15 minutes of phonemic blending, segmenting (including segment-to-spell, described in Chapter 3), and decoding instruction on individual words (based on procedures described in Chapters 4, 5, and 7) and 15 minutes of reading, rereading, and discussing connected text. Students in both treatments outperformed the control condition, and strong gains were made in word identification in both treatments. When all of the students were included in the analysis, the only significant difference in outcomes between the differing levels of text was in reading fluency, which favored students who read material at their instructional level. Students who began the study reading fewer than 50 wpm, made reliably stronger gains in all aspects of reading (words, comprehension, and fluency) when they used materials at their instructional level. The authors concluded that level of text was particularly important for the poorest readers, who, in this study, were also those who had been formally identified for special education.

Corrective Reading

Corrective Reading (Engelmann et al., 1988) has been a popular reading program for older students who read very poorly for many years. It was designed for and is marketed to poor readers in grade 4 and above. The program progresses through three levels and can be used with students who begin the program with almost no functional reading ability. Corrective Reading can be used with small groups of students, as well as one-on-one. The approach begins with phonics and blending letter sounds, and each lesson on reading words is followed by reading practice on a short story that incorporates the taught sounds and words. Sounds are taught in isolation and then in words. Word lists are practiced, students are taught key vocabulary meanings, students read and reread text to build fluency, and teachers ask comprehension questions and provide assistance for students who have difficulty finding information in the text. Positive effects on word recognition, reading fluency, and reading comprehension have been found in experimental studies (Lloyd, Cullinan, Heins, & Epstein, 1980; Polloway, Epstein, Polloway, Patton, & Ball, 1986). The program can be used as a decoding/fluency strand or can be combined with a more intensive program that incorporates strategies for reading comprehension.

Recently, Corrective Reading has been combined with Spelling Through Morphographs, and Reasoning and Writing in a 2.5-hour package for students in grade 4 and above. The REACH System (Scholastic, Inc., 2002; see Appendix A) combines a structured phonics approach with the study of morphemes for longer words, practice reading connected text in stories, fluency development, and thinking about content. This combined approach follows many of the current recommendations, but REACH has not received much research attention as an integrated package, nor has the effect of each component been evaluated for its contribution to the package.

Abbott and Berninger (1999) questioned whether the decoding component of Corrective Reading was sufficient to develop elaborated strategies for longer words, and so they tested the effects of two instructional packages on the word identification of fourth- through seventh-grade students with reading disabilities. Both treatments included phonemic blending and segmenting, decoding, and reading connected text, and were delivered through weekly 1-hour one-on-one tutorials. They differed in the fourth component, which in one treatment was 15 minutes of study skills instruction and in the other was structural analysis of individual words, which included syllable and morpheme patterns common in single and multisyllabic words. Their structural-analysis instruction was drawn from Henry's (1990) Words curriculum and the decoding instruction from Corrective Reading (Decoding B1, B2, C) (Engelmann et al., 1988). Although the trend appeared to favor students who received structural analysis, no reliable difference was found between the treatments. Both packages produced strong gains in word recognition and spelling following just 16 hours of instruction (ES > .3). Clearly, more than 16 hours will be needed to bring very low-skilled older students into comfortable facility with reading, but the study demonstrated the boost that phonics instruction provides to older students' ability to read words.

READ 180

Among the promising programs for secondary students, READ 180 (Hasslebring, 1999; see Appendix A) combines software with teacher instruction to improve word identification, fluency, and content area learning for middle and high school students who read poorly. Based on principles of anchored instruction, students view a brief video on CD-ROM that contains background information relevant to the passages they will read. They listen to a taped model of fluent reading as they follow along in the text. Then, they read the passage independently. Teachers direct word study, vocabulary, and comprehension lessons in small groups. Other reading materials for independent reading are selected from lists matched to the student's current reading ability based on the Lexile Reading Framework, and students take quizzes on computers to assess comprehension of these materials. Although only a few studies have been conducted on this system to date (Goin, Hasselbring, & McAfee, 2004; Hasselbring & Goin, 2004), the results have been positive and the content-area reading materials may help to provide age-appropriate word knowledge to students who have difficulty reading grade-level text materials.

INTEGRATING READING AND SPELLING TO PROMOTE WORD RECOGNITION AND MORE

Integrating the teaching of reading and spelling is standard practice in the primary grades as students begin to learn the letter sounds. It is much less common in the intermediate grades, perhaps because students are expected to master the basic spelling patterns by that time. To determine the relative effects of combined reading and spelling across grades for poor readers, Rashotte, MacPhee, and Torgesen (2001) taught students across grades 1–6 for 8 weeks, 50 minutes a day, in the Spell Read program in which tutors spent 30 minutes instructing students in the phonemic structure of words, 15 minutes in shared reading of connected text, and 5–6 minutes in free writing. During the phonics section of the lessons, students learned sounds for single consonants and vowels and spelled real and nonsense words, first with two sounds, then with three. Not only did students make significant gains in word recognition in this 8-week program relative to control groups, there again was no significant age effect, indicating that older students benefited as much as younger poor readers.

Language! (Greene & Woods, 2000; see Appendix A) combines the phonemic awareness and phonics aspects of print recommended for younger students with the word-study features (syllable types, affixes, and morphemes) recommended for older students, along with spelling and fluency activities. Although based on well-researched principles of word study, only limited research on the instructional package has been published (Greene, 1996). Evaluations by school districts that have used the program with middle and high school poor readers have been positive.

In sum, many studies have now shown that older students respond well to interventions in word recognition when they are of sufficient duration and intensity. Common elements across these programs include starting over with segmenting speech sounds in words and blending letter sounds and letter patterns for students who did not learn these skills in the earlier grades. Strategies for decoding multisyllabic words were also included in most of these treatments, along with practice applying acquired word-reading strategies in connected text at a level commensurate with students' decoding ability.

The focus on the phonics and letter patterns that their peers have already learned suggests several additional features of effective instruction for older poor readers. Instruction will need to be delivered in very small groups or through individual tutoring, which can be difficult to manage in a general education environment. Like younger students, older poor readers continue to need extensive practice and repetition of the skills being taught. This extensive practice may mean extending the time available for reading instruction and offering it daily for several months or years. Older poor readers also need text materials that are written at accessible levels of difficulty, which means at a level below those used by typical readers in the upper grades. Finding text materials that are age appropriate and scaled at a level low enough for poor readers to read provides another significant challenge for reading teachers.

APPENDIX A

Resources

CHAPTERS 2 AND 3: RESOURCES FOR PHONEMIC AWARENESS AND THE ALPHABETIC PRINCIPLE

Adams, M. J., Foorman, B. R., Lundberg, I., & Beeler, T. (1997). *Phonemic awareness in young children: A classroom curriculum*. Baltimore: Brookes.

Blachman, B. A., Ball, E. W., Black, R., & Tangel, D. M. (2000) *Road to the code*. Baltimore: Brookes.

O'Connor, R. E., Notari-Syverson, A., & Vadasy, P. F. (2005). *Ladders to literacy: A kindergarten activity book* (2nd ed.). Baltimore: Brookes.

CHAPTER 6: RESOURCES FOR SIGHT WORDS

Carroll, B., Davies, P., & Richman, B. (1972). *The American Heritage word frequency book*. Boston: Houghton Mifflin.

Fry, E. B., Kress, J. E., & Fountoukidis, D. L. (1993). *The reading teacher's book of lists*. Paramus, NJ: Prentice Hall.

CHAPTER 7: RESOURCES FOR READING MULTISYLLABLE WORDS

Wilson, B. (1988). *The Wilson reading system*. Millbury, MA: Wilson Language Training.

CHAPTER 9: RESOURCES FOR READING PROGRAMS
FOR OLDER POOR READERS

Engelmann, S., & Bruner, E. (1988). *Reading mastery.* Chicago: Science Research Associates.

Engelmann, S., Johnson, G., Carnine, L., Meyer, L., Becker, W., & Eisele, J. (1988). *Corrective reading skill applications (decoding B1, B2, and C).* Chicago: Science Research Associates.

Glass, G. G. (1973). *Glass analysis for decoding only.* Wood Dale, IL: Stoelting.

Greene, J. F., & Woods, J. F. (2000). *Language!* Longmont, CO: Sopris West.

Hasslebring, T. (1999). *READ 180.* New York: Scholastic.

Lindamood, C., & Lindamood, P. (1998). *Lindamood Phoneme Sequencing Program (LiPS).* San Luis Obispo, CA: Gander Publishing.

Scholastic, Inc. (2002). *The REACH System.* New York: SRA, McGraw-Hill.

APPENDIX B

Reproducible Forms and Checklists

INFORMAL SEGMENTING ASSESSMENT

In the checklist below, award 1 point for each correct phoneme in the word, so that 3 points are possible for each word. When the child can say most of the phonemes correctly in the list of words, he or she has mastered the segmenting task.

Example 1: "I can say all the sounds in *pop*. Watch me (*Touches the table top for each sound*): /p/ - /o/ - /p/. Can you do that?" [Wait for child to repeat the sounds. If the child has difficulty, say: "Do it with me. /p/ - /o/ - /p/."]

Example 2: "What sounds do you hear in *rim*?" [Wait for child to say the sounds. If the child has difficulty, say: "Do it with me. /r/ - /i/ - /m/."]

1. soap _____	2. van _____
3. top _____	4. lake _____
5. fat _____	6. mutt _____
7. dot _____	8. set _____
9. knit _____	10. gone _____

CHECKLIST OF LETTER PATTERNS THAT OCCUR
IN THE 100 MOST COMMON WORDS

Students	th	or	wh	ch	ee	al	ou	er	ar

CHECKLIST FOR LETTER–SOUND KNOWLEDGE, FORM A

Name _____   Date _____

C	f	m	b	l	e	r	t	h	u
O	p	a	k	w	j	q	n	i	x
G	v	s	y	d	z	E	I	D	L
B	J	G	N	P	A	S	R	M	F
O	Z	K	V	H	T	C	U	Y	X
W	Q								

CHECKLIST FOR LETTER–SOUND KNOWLEDGE, FORM B

Name _____ Date _____

F	c	i	p	v	a	m	x	e	j
L	u	g	y	b	x	q	h	s	o
T	d	r	k	n	z	E	Y	C	L
D	J	Q	A	N	W	P	I	M	B
K	X	O	U	H	R	T	F	Z	V
S	G					'			

CHECKLIST OF THE LETTER PATTERNS
WITH REGULAR PRONUNCIATIONS

Teachers can use this grid to determine which sounds students already know for instructional purposes. It can also be used every week or two to monitor students' progress toward learning to identify the sounds quickly.

Student _____ Date _____

th	al	ow	ing	ai	ur	oi
or	ou	ar	oy	oo	ai	qu
ee	er	oo	ir	aw	igh	ur
wh	ay	sh	ow	oa	au	ph
ch	ea	ol	igh	oi	kn	wr

COMMONLY OCCURRING WORDS IN PRINTED ENGLISH

Words 1–50   Student _____ Date _____

the	he	be	not	your
of	for	this	but	which
and	was	from	what	their
a	on	I	all	said
to	are	have	were	if
in	as	or	when	do
is	with	by	we	will
you	his	one	there	each
that	they	had	can	about
it	at	sat	an	how

Words 51–100   Student _____ Date _____

up	into	no	made	don't
out	has	make	over	didn't
then	more	than	did	water
she	her	first	down	long
many	two	been	only	little
some	like	its	way	very
so	him	who	find	after
these	see	now	use	word
would	time	people	may	called
then	could	my	other	just

(continued)

COMMONLY OCCURRING WORDS IN PRINTED ENGLISH *(page 2 of 2)*

Words 101–150   Student _____ Date _____

where	new	right	three	here
most	write	look	words	take
know	our	got	must	why
get	used	think	because	things
through	me	also	does	help
back	man	around	part	put
much	too	another	even	years
before	any	came	place	different
go	day	come	well	away
good	same	work	such	again

Words 151–200   Student _____ Date _____

off	small	line	us	saw
went	every	mother	left	something
old	found	set	end	thought
number	big	world	along	both
side	still	own	while	few
great	name	under	sound	those
tell	should	last	house	school
men	home	read	might	show
between	give	never	next	always
say	air	am	below	looked

BINGO WITH THE 25 MOST COMMON WORDS

the	of	and	a	to
in	is	you	that	it
he	for	was	on	are
as	with	his	they	at
be	this	from	I	have

is	the	he	with	was
are	in	they	to	from
at	as	of	on	be
and	this	I	you	a
it	have	that	his	for

(continued)

on	they	the	to	are
a	be	for	I	and
is	his	of	he	as
it	was	this	that	you
at	have	in	from	with

they	is	you	as	with
it	of	in	be	have
an	his	a	for	I
on	he	from	that	this
is	to	at	the	are

A CLASS CHART FOR MONITORING PROGRESS IN READING RATE

Record the number of words correct over the number of errors.

Fluency Record   Teacher _____

Date Students and text										

References

Abbott, S. P., & Berninger, V. W. (1999). It's never too late to remediate: Teaching word recognition to students with reading disabilities in Grades 4–7. *Annals of Dyslexia, 49*, 223–250.

Adams, M. (1990). *Beginning to read: Thinking and learning about print.* Cambridge, MA: MIT Press.

Adams, M. J., Foorman, B. R., Lundberg, I., & Beeler, T. (1997). *Phonemic awareness in young children: A classroom curriculum.* Baltimore: Brookes.

Adger, C. T., Hoyle, S. M., & Dickinson, D. K. (2004). Locating learning in in-service education for preschool teachers. *American Educational Research Journal, 41*, 867–900.

Allington, R. (2001). *What really matters for struggling readers?: Designing research-based programs.* New York: Longman.

Anderson, R. C., Wilson, P. T., & Fielding, L. G. (1988). Growth in reading and how children spend their time outside of school. *Reading Research Quarterly, 27*, 334–345.

Arter, J., & Jenkins, J. R. (1979). Differential-diagnosis-prescriptive teaching: A critical appraisal. *Review of Educational Research, 49*, 517–555.

Ball, E., & Blachman, B. (1991). Does phoneme awareness training in kindergarten make a difference in early word recognition and developmental spelling? *Reading Research Quarterly, 26*, 49–66.

Beck, I., & Hamilton, R. (2000). *Beginning reading module.* Washington, DC: American Federation of Teachers.

Beck, I., & McKeown, M. G. (2001). Text talk: Capturing the benefits of read-aloud experiences for young children. *The Reading Teacher, 55*, 10–20.

Beers, J. W., & Henderson, E. H. (1977). A study of developing orthographic concepts among first grade children. *Research in the Teaching of English, 11*, 133–148.

Bennett, K., Weigel, D., & Martin, S. (2002). Children's acquisition of early literacy skills: Examining family contributions. *Early Childhood Research Quarterly, 17*, 295–317.

Biemiller, A. (1977–78). Relationships between oral reading rates for letters, words, and simple text in the development of reading achievement. *Reading Research Quarterly, 13,* 223–253.

Blachman, B. A., Ball, E. W., Black, R., & Tangel, D. M. (2000) *Road to the code.* Baltimore: Brookes.

Booth, J. R., & Perfetti, C. (2002). Onset and rime structure influences naming but not early word identification in children and adults. *Scientific Studies of Reading, 6,* 1–13.

Bos, C. S., Mather, N., Silver-Pacuilla, H., & Narr, R. (2000). Learning to teach literacy skills collaboratively. *Teaching Exceptional Children, 32,* 38–45.

Brabham, E. G., & Lynch-Brown, C. (2002). Effects of teachers' reading aloud styles on vocabulary acquisition and comprehension of students in the early elementary grades. *Journal of Educational Psychology, 94,* 465–473.

Bradley, J. (1975). *Sight word association procedure.* Unpublished manuscript. College of Education, University of Arizona, Tucson.

Bradley, L., & Bryant, P. E. (1985). *Rhyme and reason in reading and spelling* (International Academy for Research in Learning Disabilities Monograph Series No. 1). Ann Arbor: University of Michigan Press.

Brady, S., Fowler, A., Stone, B., & Winburg, N. (1994). Training phonological awareness: A study with inner-city kindergarten children. *Annals of Dyslexia, 44,* 26–59.

Bus, A. G. (2001). Early book reading experience in the family: A route to literacy. In S. Neuman & D. Dickinson (Eds.), *Handbook of early literacy research, Vol. 1* (pp. 179–191). New York: Guilford Press.

Bus, A. G., Belsky, J., van IJzendoorn, M. H., & Crnik, K. (1997). Attachment and book-reading patterns: A study of mothers, fathers, and their toddlers. *Early Childhood Research Quarterly, 12,* 81–98.

Bus, A. G., van IJzendoorn, M. H., & Pellegrini, A. D. (1995). Joint book reading makes for success in learning to read: A meta-analysis on intergenerational transmission of literacy. *Review of Educational Research, 65,* 1–21.

Byrne, B., & Fielding-Barnsley, R., (1991). Evaluation of a program to teach phonemic awareness to young children. *Journal of Educational Psychology, 83,* 451–455.

Calfee, R., Lindamood, P., & Lindamood, C. (1973). Acoustic-phonetic skills and reading: Kindergarten through twelfth grade. *Journal of Educational Psychology, 64,* 293–298.

Carlisle, J. (1987). The use of morphological knowledge in spelling derived forms by learning disabled and normal students. *Annals of Dyslexia, 37,* 90–108.

Carlisle, J. (2004). Morphological processes that influence learning to read. In A. Stone, E. Silliman, B. Ehren, & K. Apel (Eds.), *Handbook of language and literacy: Development and disorders* (pp. 318–339). New York: Guilford Press.

Carnine, D. (1976). Effects of two teacher presenhtation rates on off-task behavior, answering correctly, and participation. *Journal of Applied Behavior Analysis, 9,* 199–206.

Carnine, D. (1977). Phonics versus look-say: Transfer to new words. *The Reading Teacher, 30,* 636–640.

Carnine, D., Silbert, J., & Kame'enui, E. (1997). *Direct Instruction Reading* (3rd ed.). New York: Merrill.

Caroll, B., Davies, P., & Richman, B. (1972). *The American Heritage word frequency book.* Boston: Houghton Mifflin.

Carver, R. P. (2003). The highly lawful relationships among pseudoword decoding, word identification, spelling, listening, and reading. *Scientific Studies of Reading, 7,* 127–154.

Castagnozzi, P. (1996). *Sight words you can see*. East Weymouth, MA: Castagnozzi Learning Materials.

Catts, H. W., Fey, M. E., Zhang, X., & Tomblin, J. B. (1999). Language basis of reading and reading disabilities: Evidence from a longitudinal investigation. *Scientific Studies of Reading, 3*, 331–362.

Catts, H. W., & Kamhi, A. G. (1999). *Language and reading disabilities*. Boston: Allyn & Bacon.

Center for Academic Reading Skills. (1999). *Texas primary reading inventory*. Houston: Texas Education Agency.

Chall, J. S. (1967). *Learning to read: The great debate*. New York: McGraw-Hill.

Chall, J. S. (1996). *Stages of reading development* (2nd ed.). Fort Worth, TX: Harcourt-Brace.

Christensen, C. A., & Bowey, J. A. (2005). The efficacy of orthographic rime, grapheme-phoneme correspondence, and implicit phonics approaches to teaching decoding skills. *Scientific Studies of Reading, 9*, 327–349.

Clark, E. V. (1992). Later lexical development and word formation. In P. Fletcher & B. MacWhinney (Eds.), *The handbook of child language* (pp. 393–412). Oxford, UK: Blackwell.

Clarke, L. K. (1988). Invented versus traditional spelling in first graders' writings: Effects on learning to spell and read. *Research in the Teaching of English, 22*, 281–309.

Coleman-Martin, M. B., & Heller, K. (2004). Using a modified constant prompt-delay procedure to teach spelling to students with physical disabilities. *Journal of Applied Behavior Analysis, 37*, 469–480.

Compton, D. L. (2000). Modeling the response of normally achieving and at-risk first-grade children to word reading instruction. *Annals of Dyslexia, 50*, 53–84.

Connor, C. M., Morrison, F. J., & Katch, L. E. (2004). Beyond the reading wars: Exploring the effect of child-instruction interactions on growth in early reading. *Scientific Studies of Reading, 8*, 305–336.

Council for Exceptional Children. (2003). A focus on class-wide peer tutoring. *Current Practice Alerts*, Issue 8.

Cox, A. R. (1992). *Structures and techniques: Multisensory teaching of basic written English language skills* (Alphabetic Phonics). Cambridge, MA: Educators Publishing Service.

Cunningham, P. M. (1998). The multisyllabic word dilemma: Helping students build meaning, spell, and read "big" words. *Reading and Writing Quarterly, 14*, 189–219.

Darling-Hammond, L. (2000). Teacher quality and student achievement: A review of state policy evidence. *Education and Policy Analysis Archives, 8*(1). Available online at epaa.asu.edu/epaa/v8n1

Dearing, E., McCartney, K., & Taylor, B. A. (2001). Change in family income-to-needs matters more for children with less. *Child Development, 72*, 1779–1793.

Delquadri, J., Greenwood, C., Stetton, K., & Hall, R. (1983). The peer-tutoring game: A classroom procedure for increasing opportunity to respond and spelling performance. *Education and Treatment of Children, 6*, 225–239.

Dickinson, D. K. (2001). Putting the pieces together: The impact of preschool on children's language and literacy development in kindergarten. In D. K. Dickinson & P. O. Tabors (Eds.), *Beginning literacy with language: Young children learning at home and school* (pp. 175–203). Baltimore: Brookes.

Dickinson, D. K., & Tabors, P. O. (2001). *Beginning literacy with language: Young children learning at home and school*. Baltimore: Brookes.

Dixon, R., & Engelmann, S. (1980). *Corrective spelling through morphographs*. Blacklick, OH: Science Research Associates.

Dowhower, S. L. (1987). Effects of repeated reading on second-grade transitional readers' fluency and comprehension. *Reading Research Quarterly, 22,* 389–406.

Ehri, L. (1995). Phases of development in learning to read words. *Journal of Research in Reading, 18,* 116–125.

Ehri, L. (2005). Learning to read words: Theory, findings, and issues. *Scientific Studies of Reading, 9,* 167–188.

Ehri, L., & McCormick, S. (1998). Phases of word learning: Implications for instruction with delayed and disabled readers. *Reading and Writing Quarterly: Overcoming Learning Difficulties, 14,* 135–163.

Ehri, L., & Robbins, C. (1992). Beginners need some decoding skill to read by analogy. *Reading Research Quarterly, 27,* 12–26.

Ehri, L., & Saltmarsh, J. (1995). Beginning readers outperform older disabled readers in learning to read words by sight. *Reading and Writing: An Interdisciplinary Journal, 7,* 295–326.

Ehri, L., & Wilce, L. S. (1985). Movement into reading: Is the first stage of printed word learning visual or phonetic? *Reading Research Quarterly, 20,* 163–179.

Elkonin, D. B. (1973). USSR. In J. Downing (Ed.), *Comparative reading: Cross-national studies of behavior and processes in reading and writing* (pp. 551–579). New York: MacMillan.

Engelmann, S., & Bruner, E. (1995). *Reading Mastery I, Rainbow edition.* Worthington, OH: SRA/McGraw-Hill.

Engelmann, S., Johnson, G., Carnine, D., Meyer, L., Becker, W., & Eisele, J. (1988). *Corrective reading decoding strategies.* Chicago: Macmillan/McGraw-Hill.

Fayne, H. R., & Bryant, N. D. (1981). Relative effects of various word synthesis strategies on the phonics achievement of learning disabled youngsters. *Journal of Educational Psychology, 73,* 616–623.

Fleischer, L. S., Jenkins, J. R., & Pany, D. (1979). Effects on poor readers' comprehension of training in rapid decoding. *Reading Research Quarterly, 14,* 30–48.

Foorman, B. (1995). Practiced connections of orthographic and phonological processing. In V. Berninger (Ed.), *The varieties of orthographic knowledge: Vol. II. Relationships to phonology, reading and writing* (pp. 377–418). Boston: Kluwer.

Foorman, B. R., Francis, D. J., Fletcher, J. M., Schatschneider, C., & Mehta, P. (1998). The role of instruction in learning to read: Preventing reading failure in at-risk children. *Journal of Educational Psychology, 90,* 37–55.

Freeman, D. (1978). *A pocket for Corduroy.* New York: Puffin Books.

Fry, E., Kress, J., & Fountoukidis, D. (2000). *The reading teacher's book of lists.* Paramus, NJ: Prentice-Hall.

Fuchs, D., Fuchs, L. S., Mathes, P. G., & Simmons, D. C. (1997). Peer-assisted learning strategies: Making classrooms more responsive to diversity. *American Educational Research Journal, 34,* 174–206.

Fuchs, D., Fuchs, L. S., Thompson, A., Svenson, E., Yen, L., Al Otaiba, S., et al. (2001). Peer-assisted learning strategies in reading: Extensions for kindergarten, first grade, and high school. *Remedial and Special Education, 22,* 15–21.

Gaskins, I. W., Downer, M. A., Anderson, R. C., Cunningham, P. M., Gaskins, R. W., Schommer, M., et al. (1988). A metacognitive approach to phonics: Using what you know to decode what you don't know. *Remedial and Special Education, 9,* 36–41, 66.

Gersten, R., Darch, C., & Gleason, M. (1988). Effectiveness of a direct instruction academic kindergarten for low-income students. *The Elementary School Journal, 89,* 227–240.

Gillingham, A., & Stillman, B. W. (1979). *Remedial training for children with specific disability in reading, spelling, and penmanship*. Cambridge, MA: Educators Publishing Service.

Glass, G. G. (1973). *Teaching decoding as separate from reading*. Garden City, NY: Adelphi University Press.

Gleason, M., Carnine, D., & Vala, N. (1991). Cumulative versus rapid introduction of new information. *Exceptional Children, 57*, 353–358.

Goin, L., Hasselbring, T., & McAfee, I. (2004). Executive summary, DoDEA/Scholastic READ 180 project: An evaluation of the READ 180 intervention program for struggling readers. New York: Scholastic Research and Evaluation Department.

Goldenberg, C., Reese, L., & Gallimore, R. (1992). Effects of school literacy materials on Latino children's home experiences and early reading achievement. *American Journal of Education, 100*, 497–536.

Good, R., Vollmer, M., Katz, L., & Chowdhri, S. (1993). Treatment utility of the Kaufman Assessment Battery for Children: Effects of matching instruction and students' processing strength. *School Psychology Review, 22*, 8–26.

Good, R., III, Kaminski, R., Smith, S., Laimon, D., & Dill, S. (2001). *Dynamic Indicators of Basic Early Literacy Skills*. Eugene, OR: IDEA.

Good, R. H., Simmons, D. C., & Kame'enui, E. J. (2001). The importance and decision-making utility of a continuum of fluency-based indicators of foundational reading skills for third-grade high-stakes outcomes. *Scientific Studies of Reading, 5*, 257–288.

Gough, P., & Tunmer, W. (1986). Decoding, reading, and reading disability. *Remedial and Special Education, 7*, 6–10.

Gough, P. B., & Walsh, M. (1991). Chinese, Phoenicians, and the orthographic cipher of English. In S. Brady & D. Shankweiler (Eds.), *Phonological processes in literacy* (pp. 199–209). Hillsdale, NJ: Erlbaum.

Greene, J. F. (1996). Effects of an individualized structured language curriculum. *Annals of Dyslexia, 46*, 97–121.

Greene, J. F., & Woods, J. F. (2000). *Language!* Longmont, CO: Sopris-West.

Greenwood, C., Maheady, L., & Delquadri, J. (2002). Classwide peer tutoring. In G. Stoner, M. R. Shinn, & H. Walker (Eds.), *Interventions for achievement and behavior problems* (2nd ed., pp. 611–649). Washington, DC: National Association of School Psychologists.

Greenwood, C. R., Delquadri, J. C., & Hall, R. V. (1989). Longitudinal effects of Classwide Peer Tutoring. *Journal of Educational Psychology, 81*, 371–383.

Hanna, P. R., Hanna, J. S., Hodges, R. E., & Rudorf, E. H., Jr. (1966). *Phoneme–grapheme correspondences as cues to spelling improvement* (USDOE Publication No. 32008). Washington, DC: U.S. Government Printing Office.

Hargrave, A. C., & Senechal, M. (2000). A book reading intervention with preschool children who have limited vocabularies: The benefits of regular reading and dialogic reading. *Early Childhood Research Quarterly, 15*, 75–90.

Hart, B., & Risley, T. R. (1995). *Meaningful differences in the everyday experience of young American children*. Baltimore: Brookes.

Hasselbring, T. (1999). *READ 180*. New York: Scholastic.

Hasselbring, T., & Goin, L. (2004). Literacy instruction for older struggling readers: What is the role of technology? *Reading and Writing Quarterly, 20* (3), 123–144.

Herman, P. (1985). The effect of repeated readings on reading rate, speech pauses, and word recognition accuracy. *Reading Research Quarterly, 20*, 553–565.

Hillerich, R. (1978). *A writing vocabulary of elementary children*. Springfield, IL: Thomas.

Hoover, W., & Gough, P. (1990). The simple view of reading. *Reading and Writing: An Inter-disciplinary Journal, 2,* 127–160.

Hughes, M., & Searle, D. (1997). *The violent e and other tricky sounds: Learning to spell from kindergarten through grade 6.* York, ME: Stenhouse.

Huttenlocher, J., Vasileva, M., Cymerman, E., & Levine, S. (2002). Language input and child syntax. *Cognitive Psychology, 45,* 337–374.

Jenkins, J. R, Fuchs, L. S., van den Broek, P., Espin, C., & Deno, S. L. (2003). Sources of individual differences in reading comprehension and reading fluency. *Journal of Educational Psychology, 95,* 19–29.

Juel, C. (1988). Learning to read and write: A longitudinal study of 54 children from first through fourth grades. *Journal of Educational Psychology, 80,* 437–447.

Juel, C., & Minden-Cupp, C. (2000). Learning to read words: Linguistic units and instructional strategies. *Reading Research Quarterly, 35,* 458–492.

Kame'enui, E., Stein, M., Carnine, D., & Maggs, A. (1981). Primary level word attack skills based on isolated word discrimination list and rule application training. *Reading Education, 6,* 46–55.

Kavale, K. A., & Forness, S. R. (1987). Substance over style: Assessing the efficacy of modality testing and teaching. *Exceptional Children, 54,* 228–239.

Kennedy, J., & Theobalds, P. (1987). *The teddy bears' picnic.* London: Blackie Children's Books.

Kuder, S. J. (1997). *Teaching students with language and communication disabilities.* Needham Heights, MA: Allyn & Bacon.

Kuhn, M., & Stahl, S. (2003). Fluency: A review of developmental and remedial practices. *Journal of Educational Psychology, 95,* 3–21.

LaBerge, D., & Samuels, J. (1974). Toward a theory of automatic information processing in reading. *Cognitive Psychology, 6,* 293–323.

Lenz, B. K., & Hughes, C. A. (1990). A word identification strategy for adolescents with learning disabilities. *Journal of Learning Disabilities, 23,* 149–158, 163.

Levy, B., Abello, B., & Lysynchuk, L. (1997). Transfer from word training to reading in context: Gains in reading fluency and comprehension. *Learning Disabilities Quarterly, 20,* 173–188.

Levy, B. A., Bourassa, D. C., & Horn, C. (1999). Fast and slow namers: Benefits of segmentation and whole word training. *Journal of Experimental Child Psychology, 73,* 115–138.

Liberman, I., & Shankweiler, D. (1985). Phonology and the problems of learning to read and write. *Remedial and Special Education, 6,* 8–17.

Lindamood, C., & Lindamood, P. (1975, 1984). *The ADD program: Auditory discrimination in depth.* Austin, TX: PRO-ED.

Lloyd, J., Cullinan, D., Heins, E., & Epstein, M. (1980). Direct instruction: Effects on oral and written language comprehension. *Learning Disabilities Quarterly, 3,* 70–76.

Lovett, M., Borden, S., DeLuca, T., Lacerenza, L., Benson, N., & Brackstone, D. (1994). Treating the core deficits of developmental dyslexia: Evidence of transfer of learning after phonologically and strategically based instruction to improve outcomes. *Developmental Psychology, 30,* 805–822.

Lovett, M. W., Lacerenza, L., & Borden, S. L. (2000). Putting struggling reading on the PHAST track: A program to integrate phonological and strategy-based remedial reading instruction and maximize outcomes. *Journal of Learning Disabilities, 33,* 458–476.

Lovett, M. W., Lacerenza, L., Borden, S. L., Frijiters, J. C., Steinbach, K. A., & De Palma, M. (2000). Components of effective remediation for developmental reading disability:

Combining phonological and strategy-based instruction to improve outcomes. *Journal of Educational Psychology, 92*, 263–283.

Lovett, M. W., & Steinbach, K. A. (1997). The effectiveness of remedial programs for reading disabled children of different ages: Does the benefit decrease for older children? *Learning Disabilities Quarterly, 20*, 189–210.

Lundberg, I., Frost, J., & Petersen, O. (1988). Effects of an extensive program for stimulating phonological awareness in preschool children. *Reading Research Quarterly, 23*, 263–284.

Mason, J. M. (1977). Questioning the notion of independent processing stages in reading. *Journal of Educational Psychology, 69*, 288–297.

Mather, N., & Goldstein, S. (2001). *Learning disabilities and challenging behaviors: A guide to intervention and classroom management.* Baltimore: Brookes.

Mathes, P., & Fuchs, L. S. (1993). Peer-mediated reading instruction in special education resource rooms. *Learning Disabilities Research and Practice, 8*, 233–242.

McCandliss, B., Beck, I., Sendak, R., & Perfetti, C. (2003). Focusing attention on decoding for children with poor reading skills: Design and preliminary tests of the Word Building intervention. *Scientific Studies of Reading, 7*, 75–104.

McCutchen, D., & Berninger, V. (1999). Those who know, teach well: Helping teachers master literacy-related subject matter knowledge. *Learning Disabilities Research and Practice, 14*, 215–226.

McGovern, A. (1975). *The secret soldier: The story of Deborah Sampson.* New York: Scholastic.

McKeown, M., Beck, I., Omanson, R., & Pople, M. (1985). Some effects of the nature and frequency of vocabulary instruction on the knowledge and use of words. *Reading Research Quarterly, 20*, 522–535.

Mcmaster, K. L., Fuchs, D., & Fuchs, L. S. (2006). Research on peer-assisted learning strategies: The promise and limitations of peer-mediated instruction. *Reading and Writing Quarterly, 22*, 5–25.

Mercer, C., & Campbell, K. (1998). *Great Leaps reading program.* Micanopy, FL: Diarmuid.

Metsala, J. L., & Walley, A. C. (1998). Spoken vocabulary growth and the segmental restructuring of lexical representations: Precursors to phonemic awareness and early reading ability. In J. L. Metsala & L. C. Ehri (Eds.), *Word recognition in beginning literacy* (pp. 89–120). Mahwah, NJ: Erlbaum.

Meyer, M. S., & Felton, R. H. (1999). Repeated reading to enhance fluency: Old approaches and new directions. *Annals of Dyslexia, 49*, 283–306.

Miranda, A. (1998). *Lions of the plains.* New York: Scholastic.

Moats, L. C. (2000). *Speech to print: Language essentials for teachers.* Baltimore: Brookes.

Nagy, W., Anderson, R. C., Schommer, M., Scott, J., and Stallman, A. (1989). Morphological families in the internal lexicon. *Reading Research Quarterly, 24*, 262–282.

Nation, K., Allen, R., & Hulme, C. (2001). The limitations of orthographic analogy in early reading development: Performance on the clue-word task depends on phonological priming and elementary decoding skill, not the use of orthographic analogy. *Journal of Experimental Child Psychology, 80*, 75–94.

Nation, K., & Snowling, M. (1998). Individual differences in contextual facilitation: Evidence from dyslexia and poor reading comprehension. *Child Development, 69*, 996–1011.

Nation, K., & Snowling, M. (1999). Development differences in sensitivity to semantic relations among good and poor comprehenders: Evidence from semantic priming. *Cognition, 70*, B1–B13.

National Reading Panel. (2000). *Teaching children to read: An evidence-based assessment of the scientific research literature on reading and its implications for reading instruction.* Washington, DC: National Institute of Child Health and Human Development.

National Research Council. (2002). *Minority students in special and gifted education.* Washington, DC: National Academy Press.

Nippold, M. A. (1998). *Later language development: The school-age and adolescent years.* Austin, TX: PRO-ED.

O'Connor, R. E. (2000). Increasing the intensity of intervention in kindergarten and first grade. *Learning Disabilities Research and Practice, 15,* 43–54.

O'Connor, R. E., & Bell, K. M. (2004). Teaching students with reading disability to read words. In A. Stone, E. Silliman, B. Ehren, & K. Apel (Eds.), *Handbook of language and literacy: Development and disorders* (pp. 479–496). New York: Guilford Press.

O'Connor, R. E., Bell, K. M., Harty, K. R., Larkin, L. K., Sackor, S., & Zigmond, N. (2002). Teaching reading to poor readers in the intermediate grades: A comparison of text difficulty. *Journal of Educational Psychology, 94,* 474–485.

O'Connor, R. E., Fulmer, D., Harty, K., & Bell, K. (2005). Layers of reading intervention in kindergarten through third grade: Changes in teaching and child outcomes. *Journal of Learning Disabilities, 38,* 440–455.

O'Connor, R. E., & Jenkins, J. R. (1995). Improving the generalization of sound/symbol knowledge: Teaching spelling to kindergarten children with disabilities. *Journal of Special Education, 29,* 255–275.

O'Connor, R. E., & Jenkins, J. R. (1999). The prediction of reading disabilities in kindergarten and first grade. *Scientific Studies of Reading, 3,* 159–197.

O'Connor, R. E., Jenkins, J. R., & Slocum, T. A. (1995). Transfer among phonological tasks in kindergarten: Essential instructional content. *Journal of Educational Psychology, 2,* 202–217.

O'Connor, R. E., Notari-Syverson, N., & Vadasy, P. (1996). Ladders to literacy: The effects of teacher-led phonological activities for kindergarten children with and without disabilities. *Exceptional Children, 63,* 117–130.

O'Connor, R. E., Notari-Syverson, N., & Vadasy, P. (2005). *Ladders to literacy: A kindergarten activity book.* Baltimore: Brookes.

O'Connor, R. E., & Padeliadu, S. (2000). Blending versus whole word approaches in first grade remedial reading: Short-term and delayed effects on reading and spelling words. *Reading and Writing: An Interdisciplinary Journal, 13,* 159–182.

O'Connor, J. R., & Wilson, B. A. (1995). Effectiveness of the Wilson Reading System used in public school training. In C. McIntyre & J. Pickering (Eds.), *Clinical studies of multisensory structured language education* (pp. 247–254). Salem, OR: International Multisensory Structured Language Education Council.

Owens, R. E., Jr. (1999). *Language disorders: A functional approach to assessment and intervention* (3rd ed.). New York: Merrill/Macmillan.

Palmer, J., MacLeod, C. M., Hunt, E., & Davidson, J. E. (1985). Information processing correlates of reading. *Journal of Memory and Language, 24* (1), 59–88.

Payne, A. C., Whitehurst, G., & Angell, A. (1994). The role of home literacy environment in the development of language ability in preschool children from low-income families. *Early Childhood Research Quarterly, 9,* 427–40.

Perfetti, C. A. (1985). *Reading ability.* New York: Oxford University Press.

Perfetti, C. A. (2003). The universal grammar of reading. *Scientific Studies of Reading, 7,* 3–27.

Perfetti, C. A., Beck, I., Bell, L., & Hughes, C. (1987). Phonemic knowledge and learning to read are reciprocal: A longitudinal study of first grade children. *Merrill–Palmer Quarterly, 33*, 283–319.

Perfetti, C. A., & Hart, L. (2002). The lexical quality hypothesis. In L. Verhoevern (Ed.), *Precursors of functional literacy* (pp. 189–213). Philadelphia: John Benjamins.

Pinnel, G. S., Pikulski, J. J., Wixson, K. K., Campbell, J. R., Gough, P. B., & Beatty, A. S. (1995). *Listening to children read aloud*. Washington, DC: Office of Educational Research and Improvement, U.S. Department of Education.

Polloway, E., Epstein, M., Polloway, C., Patton, J., & Ball, D. (1986). Corrective reading program: An analysis of effectiveness with learning disabled and mentally retarded students. *Remedial and Special Education, 7*, 41–47.

Rack, J. P., Snowling, M. J., & Olson, R. K. (1992). The nonword reading deficit in developmental dyslexia: A review. *Reading Research Quarterly, 27*, 29–53.

Rashotte, C. A., MacPhee, K., & Torgesen, J. K. (2001). The effectiveness of a group reading instruction program with poor readers in multiple grades. *Learning Disabilities Quarterly, 24*, 119–134.

Read, C. (1971). Preschool children's knowledge of English phonology. *Harvard Educational Review, 41*, 1–34.

Reistma, P. (1983). Printed word learning in beginning readers. *Journal of Experimental Child Psychology, 36*, 321–339.

Rupley, W. H., Willson, V. L., & Nichols, W. D. (1998). Exploration of the developmental components contributing to elementary school children's reading comprehension. *Scientific Studies of Reading, 2*, 143–158.

Samuels, S. J. (1979). The method of repeated readings. *The Reading Teacher, 32*, 403–408.

Scarborough, H. S. (1990). Very early language deficits in dyslexic children. *Child Development, 61*, 1728–1743.

Scarborough, H. S. (2001). Connecting early language and literacy to later reading (dis)abilities: Evidence, theory, and practice. In S. B. Neuman & D. K. Dickinson (Eds.), *Handbook of early literacy research* (pp. 97–110). New York: Guilford Press.

Schatschneider, C. (2004). *Predicting reading comprehension: A study of third-, seventh-, and tenth-grade students*. Paper presented at the Florida Center for Reading Research Conference on Vocabulary and Reading. Captiva Island, FL.

Scholastic, Inc. (2002). *The REACH System*. New York: SRA, McGraw-Hill.

Seeger, P., & Hays, M. (1986). *Abiyoyo*. New York: Aladdin Books.

Shanahan, T. (1980). The impact of writing instruction on learning to read. *Reading World, 19*, 357–368.

Shany, M. T., & Biemiller, A. (1995). Assisted reading practice: Effects on performance for poor readers in grades 3 and 4. *Reading Research Quarterly, 30*, 382–395.

Share, D. (1995). Phonological recoding and self-teaching: Sine qua non of reading acquisition. *Cognition, 55*, 151–218.

Share, D., Jorm, A., MacLean, R., & Matthews, R. (1984). Sources of individual differences in reading acquisition. *Journal of Educational Psychology, 76*, 1309–1324.

Shaywitz, S. (2003). *Overcoming dyslexia: A new and complete science-based program for reading problems at any level*. New York: Knopf.

Shefelbine, J. (1990). A syllable-unit approach to teaching decoding of polysyllable words to fourth- and sixth-grade disabled readers. In J. Zutell & S. McCormick (Eds.), *Literacy theory and research: Analysis from multiple paradigms* (pp. 223–230). Chicago: National Reading Conference.

Simmons, D. C., Kuykendall, K., King, K., Cornachione,C., & Kame'enui, E. (2000). Implementation of a schoolwide reading improvement model: "No one ever told us it would be this hard!" *Learning Disabilities Research and Practice, 15,* 92–100.

Sindelar, P. T., Monda, L. E., & O'Shea, L. J. (1990). Effects of repeated readings on instructional- and mastery-level readers. *Journal of Educational Research, 83,* 220–226.

Slocum, T. A., O'Connor, R. E., & Jenkins, J. R. (1993). Transfer among phonological manipulation skills. *Journal of Educational Psychology, 85,* 618–630.

Snow, C., Burns, S., & Griffin, P. (1998). *Preventing reading difficulty in young children.* Washington, DC: National Academy Press.

Snow, C., Tabors, P. O., & Dickinson, D. K. (2001). Language development in the preschool years. In D. K. Dickinson & P. O. Tabors (Eds.), *Beginning literacy with language* (pp. 1–25). Baltimore: Brookes.

Snow, C., Tabors, P. O., Nicholson, P. A., & Kurland, B. F. (1995). SHELL: Oral language and early literacy skills in kindergarten and first-grade children. *Journal of Research in Childhood Education, 10,* 37–48.

Spear-Swerling, L., & Sternberg, R. (1994). The road not taken: An integrative theoretical model of reading disability. *Journal of Learning Disabilities, 27,* 91–103.

Stanovich, K. (1986). Matthew effects in reading: Some consequences of individual differences in the acquisition of literacy. *Reading Research Quarterly, 21,* 360–406.

Stanovich, K. E. (2000). *Progress in understanding reading: Scientific foundations and new frontiers.* New York: The Guilford Press.

Storch, S. A., & Whitehurst, G. J. (2002). Oral language and code-related precursors to reading: Evidence from a longitudinal structural model. *Developmental Psychology, 38,* 934–947.

Swanborn, M. S. L., & de Glopper, K. (1999). Incidental word learning while reading: A meta-analysis. *Review of Educational Research, 69,* 261–285.

Swanson, H. L. (1999). Reading research for students with LD: A meta-analysis of intervention outcomes. *Journal of Learning Disabilities, 32,* 504–532.

Swanson, H. L., & Alexander, J. E. (2000). Cognitive processes as predictors of word recognition and reading comprehension in learning-disabled and skilled readers. *Journal of Educational Psychology, 89,* 128–158.

Tangel, D. M., & Blachman, B. A. (1992). Effect of phoneme awareness instruction on kindergarten children's invented spelling. *Journal of Reading Behavior, 24,* 233–261.

Templeton, S. (1991). Teaching and learning the English spelling system: Reconceptualizing method and purpose. *Elementary School Journal, 92,* 183–199.

Torgesen, J. K. (2000). Individual differences in response to early interventions in reading: The lingering problem of treatment resisters. *Learning Disabilities Research and Practice, 15,* 55–64.

Torgesen, J. K., Alexander, A. W., Wagner, R. K., Rashotte, C. A., Voeller, K., & Conway, T. (2001). Intensive remedial instruction for children with severe reading disabilities: Immediate and long-term outcomes from two instructional approaches. *Journal of Learning Disabilities, 34,* 33–58, 78.

Torgesen, J. K., Wagner, R. K., & Rashotte, C. A. (1997). Prevention and remediation of severe reading disabilities: Keeping the end in mind. *Scientific Studies in Reading, 1,* 217–234.

Treiman, R. (1998). Why spelling?: The benefits of incorporating spelling in beginning reading instruction. In J. Metsala & L. Ehri (Eds.), *Word recognition in beginning literacy* (pp. 289–313). Mahwah, NJ: Erlbaum.

Treiman, R., & Zukowski, A. (1988). Units of reading and spelling. *Journal of Memory and Language, 27*, 466–477.

Truch, S. (1994). Stimulating basic reading processes using Auditory Discrimination in Depth. *Annals of Dyslexia, 44*, 60–80.

Tunmer, W., Herriman, M., & Nesdale, A. (1988). Metalinguistic abilities and beginning reading. *Reading Research Quarterly, 23*, 134–158.

Tunmer, W. E., & Chapman, J. W. (1998). Language prediction skill, phonological recoding ability, and beginning reading. In C. Hulme & R. M. Joshi (Eds), *Reading and spelling: Development and disorders* (pp. 33–67). Mahwah, NJ: Erlbaum.

Vadasy, P. F. (2001). Approaches to comprehension instruction. Unpublished manuscript. Seattle, WA: Washington Research Institute.

Vadasy, P. F., Jenkins, J. R., Antil, L. R., Wayne, S. K., & O'Connor, R. E. (1997). Community-based early reading intervention for at-risk first graders. *Learning Disabilities Research and Practice, 12*, 29–39.

Vadasy, P. F., Wayne, S. K., O'Connor, R. E., Jenkins, J. R., Pool, K., Firebaugh, M., et al. (2005). *Sound Partners: A tutoring program in phonics-based early reading.* Longmont, CO: Sopris West.

van Kleek, A. (2004. Fostering pre-literacy development via storybook-sharing interactions. In C. A. Stone, E. R. Silliman, B. J. Ehren, & K. Apel (Eds.), *Handbook of language and literacy* (pp. 175–208). New York: Guilford Press.

Vaughn, S. (2003, December). How many tiers are needed for response to intervention to achieve acceptable prevention outcomes. Paper presented at the National Research Center on Learning Disabilities "Response to Intervention" Symposium, Kansas City, MO.

Vaughn, S., Moody, S. W., & Schumm, J. S. (1998). Broken promises: Reading instruction in the resource room. *Exceptional Children, 64*, 211–225.

Vellutino, F., & Scanlon, D. (1987). Phonological coding, phonological awareness, and reading ability: Evidence from a longitudinal and experimental study. *Merrill-Palmer Quarterly, 33*, 321–363.

Venezky, R. (1999). *The American way of spelling: The structure and origins of American English orthography.* New York: Guilford Press.

Wagner, R., Torgesen, J., & Rashotte, C. (1999). *Comprehensive Test of Phonological Processing.* Austin, TX: PRO-ED.

Weizman, Z., & Snow, C. (2001). Lexical input as related to children's vocabulary acquisition: Effects of sophisticated exposure and support for meaning. *Developmental Psychology, 37*, 265–279.

Wells, G. (1985). Preschool literacy-related activities and success in school. In D. R. Olson, N. Torrance, & A. Hildyard (Eds.), *Literacy, language and learning: The nature and consequences of reading and writing* (pp. 229–255). New York: Cambridge University Press.

White, T., Power, M., & White, S. (1989). Morphological analysis: Implications for teaching and understanding vocabulary growth. *Reading Research Quarterly, 24*, 283–304.

White, T., Sowell, J., & Yanagihara, A. (1989). Teaching elementary students to use word-part cues. *The Reading Teacher, 42*, 302–308.

Whitehurst, G. J., Falco, F. L., Lonigan, C., Fischel, J. E., DeBaryshe, B. D., Valdez-Menchaca, M. C., et al. (1988). Accelerating language development through picture-book reading. *Developmental Psychology, 24*, 552–558.

Williams, J. (1980). Teaching decoding with an emphasis on phoneme analysis and phoneme blending. *Journal of Educational Psychology, 72*, 1–15.

Wilson, B. (1988). *The Wilson Reading System*. Millbury, MA: Wilson Language Training.

Wise, B. W., Ring, J., & Olson, R. K. (2000). Individual differences in gains from computer-assisted remedial reading. *Journal of Experimental Child Psychology, 77*, 198–235.

Wolery, M. (2002). Embedding and distributing constant time delay in circle time and transitions. *Topics in Early Childhood Special Education, 22*, 14–25.

Wolery, M., Holcombe, A., Cybriwsky, C., Doyle, O., Schuster, J., Ault, M., et al. (1992). Constant time delay with discrete responses: A review of effectiveness and demographic, procedural, and methodological parameters. *Research on Developmental Disabilities, 13*, 239–266.

Wolf, M., & Bowers, P. G. (1999). The double-deficit hypothesis for the developmental dyslexia. *Journal of Educational Psychology, 91*, 415–438.

Yopp, H. (1988). The validity and reliability of phonemic awareness tests. *Reading Research Quarterly, 23*, 159–177.

Young, A. R., Bowers, P. G., & MacKinnon, G. E. (1996). Effects of prosodic modeling and repeated reading on poor readers' fluency and comprehension. *Applied Psycholinguistics, 17*, 59–84.

Zeno, S., Ivens, S., Millard, R., & Duvvuri, R. (1995). *The educator's word frequency guide*. Brewster, NY: Applied Science Associates.

Index